The Cold War
in Welfare

The Cold War in Welfare

Stock Markets versus Pensions

———◆———

RICHARD MINNS

VERSO

London • New York

First published by Verso 2001
© Richard Minns 2001
All rights reserved

Verso
UK: 6 Meard Street, London W1V 3HR
USA: 180 Varick Street, New York NY 10014–4606

Verso is the imprint of New Left Books
www.versobooks.com

ISBN 1–85984–625–4

British Library Cataloguing in Publication Data
A catalogue record for this book is available from the British Library

Library of Congress Cataloging-in-Publication Data
Minns, Richard.
    The cold war in welfare: stock markets versus pensions/
Richard Minns.
        p. cm.
    Includes bibliographical references and index.
    ISBN 1-85984-625-4 (cloth)
    1. Pension trusts—Investments. 2. Public welfare—
Finance. 3. Pension trusts—Investments—United States.
4. Public welfare—United States—Finance. 5. Pension
trusts—Investments—Great Britain. 6. Public welfare—
Great Britain— Finance. 7. Pension trusts—
Investments—Commonwealth countries. 8. Public
welfare—Commonwealth countries—Finance. I. Title.

HD7105.4.M56 2001
331.25′2—dc21   00–054984

Typeset in New Baskerville by M Rules
Printed in Great Britain by Biddles Ltd,
Guildford and King's Lynn

Contents

Tables

Figures

Preface

A new Cold War has developed between competing blocs of countries over the role of stock markets versus the state in the provision of pensions, or social security, and the financing of the economy more generally. This new Cold War is all about conflicts over the role of the state and public expenditure, the promotion of private savings for retirement and social security, and an increase in the importance of capital markets for financing both social security/pensions *and* the corporate sector. The 'globalisation' of financial markets has, it seems, less to do with the onward march of objective technical forces that can provide us with better pensions and economic growth than with the extension of one particular, Anglo-American model of a financial system.

The growth of financial markets after the Second World War was underpinned by the phenomena of Eurodollars and petrodollars. After these came 'pension dollars', people's private savings for retirement, representing over $12,000 billion in worldwide assets – more than the combined value of all the companies quoted on the world's three largest stock markets. There is enormous pressure to increase this figure further as public pension systems are said to be both 'in crisis' and a 'burden' on national economic growth because of rising costs for taxpayers, employees and corporations. The crisis is said to be attributable in part to ageing populations throughout the world, but also to the fact that governments are taken to be inefficient and unproductive, while the financial markets are apparently not.

The argument in this book is threefold. First, I will suggest that we have underestimated the link between the nature of pension systems and their accompanying financial systems – stock markets or their alternatives. If there is a stock-market approach to the financing or control of industry and the alleged promotion of economic growth, then there will be a stock-market approach to pensions/social security. If there is a greater reliance on banks and interlocking corporate structures in the economic or business spheres, there will be a much smaller role for stock-market-based social security provision in the social sphere. There is, in other words, a clear link between the nature of the financial system and, first, its relationship with companies, and, second, the funding of welfare/social security.

Second, I will propose that the argument for the extension of private provision of pensions/social security is not really about pensions as such, but about the extension and growth of stock markets and 'liberalised' financial markets. If pensions and the 'burden' of ageing populations on state expenditure were not the topical issues, it would probably be something else which would help to increase the role of capital markets.

Third, I will argue that, whatever we now define as 'socialism', 'social welfare', 'social security' or 'welfare state', the case for stock markets as an alternative means of social protection has not been proven. There are many fundamental problems with its logic and with the evidence which is produced to back up its assumptions. In other words, the stock-market model of pensions, investment and economic growth is unpersuasive in terms of providing the economic and social benefits which it promises.

But why does the argument for privatisation of pensions through stock-market investment persist? Although the details are sometimes apparently complex, I will tentatively suggest that there are financial, commercial, political *and* labour interests involved, backed up by extensive academic arguments, which are frequently concerned with priorities other than pensions. Some of the arguments have persisted for more than thirty years. Perhaps we should refer not to the 'old-age crisis', as the World Bank and the press continually do, but to the 'age-old crisis'!

Indeed, the stock-market model has received significant endorsement from the World Bank. In 1994, the Bank produced a report, *Averting the Old Age Crisis*, on the future of pensions and their relationship to the promotion of economic growth (World Bank, 1994), which has often been quoted and used by academics, policy advisers, politicians and the press. The report contained analyses of different pension systems and it recommended that for most countries there should be a predominantly or significantly greater, private structure of pension savings and investment which would operate through stock markets. Not only would this protect retirement provision; it would also, as emphasised in the subtitle to the report (Policies to Protect the Old *and* Promote Growth), promote economic growth – the crucial link again being the role of stock markets.

It is not just the World Bank which has been promoting the case for greater privatisation of pensions in various countries or, in American terms, the privatisation of social security provision. A wide range of individuals and institutions, drawn from various backgrounds – and offering variations on the same basic theme – support the general argument which favours private provision of old-age pensions through stock-market investment. They include senior academics from the US and the UK, who agree that the role of the state should be restricted in pensions provision. Such a reduction in the role of the state in social policy would decrease 'costly' public expenditure on welfare or social security, thereby, according to many arguments, once again enhancing economic growth and making the support for old-age pensions more sustainable.

The advocates of privatisation are also supported by the financial press, who often have an influential role in social change or in influencing public opinion on such issues. They frequently echo the gloomy warnings of 'bankruptcy' that are said to follow from the continuing role of the public sector and from the proverbial ticking clock of demographic 'time bombs'. In the UK and elsewhere the *Financial Times*, for example, has been an important publisher of articles which, on balance, implicitly or explicitly support the case for greater private provision through funded or invested schemes which rely on investments through capital markets. Many of its articles on the subject contain tendentious language such as 'burdens', 'shake-ups', and 'time bombs'. In the US, papers such as *The New York Times* and the *Wall Street Journal* have given interesting commentaries on changes in pension systems. But they still appear, on balance, to advocate, whether deliberately or not, one type of system over another, echoing what appears to be a certain received wisdom – what I shall term the 'Anglo-American' privatisation model.

Last, but certainly not least, come the politicians who advise us that our savings for social protection and social security are safer and more effective for both the economy and social welfare if they are placed in the hands of private money managers, insurance companies and stock markets rather than in public institutions which would be directly accountable to, or owned by, the state. They and the reformers also argue that the funds should be less reliant on the funding of government debt and more active in the support for private equities and bonds and the promotion of the 'new risk culture'.

There have been some interesting and critical responses to the privatisation argument, many of which are referred to in this book. What the book pays special attention to, however, is the fact that the distinguishing characteristic of the privatisation argument is *the use of capital markets* for the provision of social welfare. This applies to proposals for pension reform in Western, Central and Eastern Europe, America, North and South, and just about everywhere else as proposed by the World Bank and others.

In my view, the general exhortation issued by those who support the arguments concerning the benefits of capital markets for worldwide economic development and social welfare is singularly unconvincing. The privatisation of pensions provision through the use of stock markets does *not* lead to better pensions for a wide range of people, and it does *not* lead to greater economic growth. *Privatisation is about reducing the role of the state and expanding the role of stock markets, which is altogether a different proposition.*

However unfashionable it may sound in this age of the 'post-state', 'pro-market' society of 'consumers' (as opposed to 'citizens'), my conclusion is that there is a strong case for reconsidering the effectiveness and the promotion of state, or non-stock-market-led systems of welfare and social security.

On the personal front, I would particularly like to thank Robin Blackburn and Bryn Davies for their consistent support as critics and commentators, along with numerous individuals in many countries who have provided information and comments. In addition, I would like to give thanks to staff at the WordsWorth bookshop in Camberwell, London, for responding so efficiently to all my faxes and requests from distant places for essential reading matter in connection with the writing of the book. I would finally like to acknowledge the invaluable help provided by the libraries of the London School of Economics, University College and the City Business Library, all in London, UK; and the national research library in St Petersburg, Russia.

Welfare Blocs
and Pensions

INTRODUCTION

First, a few questions.

- Are retired people just another 'burden' on the state, a 'cost' for business and working people, or is there something more positive in the relationship between them?
- Is the way we pay for people's retirement related to how we finance investment and commerce?
- What is the relationship between the payment of pensions for people in retirement and what happens on the stock market?
- Are pensions the result of what we save, or are they the result of what we produce?
- Is economic growth dependent on the nature of the social security and pension system, or is the relationship the other way around, meaning economic growth comes first, pensions provision comes second? Or are pensions primarily a social issue?
- Why do the US and the UK have large stock markets *and* large privately invested pension arrangements, while most European countries have relatively small stock markets *and* a different way of paying for pensions?

To answer these questions we need briefly to consider the range of financial and production systems on the one hand and the range of pension systems on the other. We can then consider the relationship between the two.

The basic issue is to outline how different financial systems finance productive activity, and how different pension or social security systems contribute to this. Or, conversely, we need to consider how they are allegedly a drag on the process of investment in productive activity. In other words, the aim is to establish the positive or negative contribution of many current pension and social security arrangements to their societies' distribution *and* production of wealth.

I will concentrate on some of the issues concerning pensions, and some of the concerns about corporate activity, corporate responsibility, investment and social welfare in the 'Anglo-American' model as opposed to those in the 'European' model, and will offer some comparisons with 'Asian' models of investment, production and welfare. There are many variations on the basic theme, but I will demonstrate that the fundamental issues concerning finance, industry and the payment of pensions are relatively straightforward. The division of the world into different models or 'blocs' will always raise questions about the degree of 'fit' of different countries, especially when we no longer have the competing ideologies of the old Cold War to assist us in a kind of binary system of social alternatives. But, I suggest that there *is* a structure of competing ideologies, and these basically boil down to differences over the role of stock markets in commerce *and* social welfare.

THE BASICS

We have heard of different relationships between finance and industry which are designed to promote economic growth, economic 'efficiency' or the most effective allocation of capital resources – the capital-market approach versus bank-oriented approaches (see, for instance, Rybczynski, 1988; Dore et al., 1999). Broadly speaking, there is what I shall term the Anglo-American approach, with its emphasis on the role of stock markets and the so-called free movement of capital; then there is the continental European approach, which relies on banks and interlocking corporate structures rather than stock markets as the core relationship between the financial sector and the productive sector; then Asian state centralism, also with its interlocking banks and corporate structures, along with strong state involvement in economic decision-making. These are different models of *finance and production*.

Next, we may have also read about the division of the world into different approaches to *social welfare, pensions* or *social security* (see in particular the important work of Esping-Andersen [1990] and before him Richard Titmuss in various references). These different approaches to social policies and welfare include various roles for the state and the private sector as represented, for example, by the philosophies to be found in the US and the UK on the one hand, and the various approaches of continental European countries on the other. These are contrasting philosophies about the roles of the public and private sectors in the redistribution of wealth and the provision of welfare or social security. They are different models of *finance and social redistribution*.

There is, of course, a growing recognition of a link between these two dimensions of economic development and social redistribution. The relationship between the two has led to many allegations about the cost of social provision in continental Europe and the damage to competitiveness and economic growth which this allegedly entails. Nowhere is this relationship more stark than in pensions.

Pensions, in fact, now dominate public expenditure on social welfare. Private provision of pensions has even come to be important for the development of stock markets and the broader economy. In fact, the link between welfare and financial systems, as implied in my earlier questions, has become central to arguments about pension systems. How we pay for pensions is now an important part of the debates about production, finance *and* the causes of economic growth.

At the risk of a little oversimplification, I will summarise pension systems and the associated arguments as follows.

On the one hand we have an Anglo-American philosophy of pensions, supported by international, private financial institutions and the public-sector World Bank. This philosophy proposes to freeze, contain or minimise the role of the state, in some cases relegating it to a residual tier or so-called 'pillar'. It advocates a large or even primary use of private management of investment on stock markets in order to use the alleged increase in savings more productively, thereby increasing economic growth and, consequently, creating greater resources for retirement provision.

On the other hand, there are approaches which propose a comparatively larger, or more substantial role for the state. Even if they include some role for private-sector provision, they are more reluctant to use *capital markets,* with private management of financial resources, as the predominant mechanism for addressing both economic growth and retirement provision. In fact, 'economic growth' hardly features in this analysis and prescription of welfare arrangements.

It is this conflict over the role of financial markets which makes the world's 'welfare blocs' inherently bound up with different financial systems and mechanisms for promoting investment and economic growth. In other words, the attempts to extend the Anglo-American model of pensions provision are at the same time intrinsically linked to arguments for the expansion of capital markets and their associated financial flows.

Essentially, welfare is no longer a distributional issue, or even an employment issue, which is separate from, or a counter to, broader financial and productive systems and their outcomes. *We have to consider social security and the different models of finance and production together.* All of the elements in the different approaches to social policies, financial systems and economic development are bound together. They were not previously, at least not to such an extent. Rather, social policies, in generally perceived terms, were supposed to be a counter to, or insurance against, 'the market' and its failings. In fact, the structure and financing of social policies have now become extremely important for the development of financial systems themselves as well as for the development of the market economy. I believe that this importance of welfare arrangements for financial systems and production, rather than just social redistribution, is one of the reasons why the debates about pensions and the growing numbers of old people have become so important.

THE PENSION PARAMETERS

Formal pension arrangements, where there is provision in law for their establishment and operation, for the most part have two elements – a 'basic' pension and a 'supplementary' or 'complementary' pension. The supplementary (complementary) can, in turn, be split into two parts. These are all sometimes referred to as 'pillars' – the first pillar is the basic; the second pillar is a group or universal supplementary system, often compulsory; the third is an additional, individual, voluntary, private supplementary arrangement.

Generally speaking, the basic is usually associated with the state, while the supplementary or complementary schemes are linked to some form of private provision. In addition, a basic pension can be 'flat-rate' or it can have 'earnings-related' features based on contributions (social insurance) or calculations related to lifetime earnings, or it can be financed solely or mainly from general public revenues.

A supplementary pension is usually earnings-related in one way or another. It always, so far as I can tell, features a (usually private) insurance dimension linked to contributions which inevitably are based on the ability, and increasingly with personalised, voluntary arrangements, the willingness, to pay.

Some countries have a small, basic pension run by the state and financed out of current revenue, whether from social insurance contributions or general public revenue – the state 'pay-as-you-go' system, frequently flat-rate. To supplement this, and in some cases to minimise or even replace it, they have significant supplementary schemes run by private financial institutions and invested on stock markets – a privately run and 'funded' system – 'funded' meaning that returns from stock-market investments which are made by prospective pensioners will help to pay towards liabilities arising from the cost of providing for them when they become pensioners.

This means that returns on the investments are intended to contribute towards the payment of pensions. Individual self-reliance is emphasised and tax concessions on contributions and investment returns are common. The basic pension is increasingly referred to as a 'safety net' to demonstrate its residual nature, or else, as in the US, as a burden on public expenditure and a curb on savings and economic growth which greater private provision and management should replace. This is the Anglo-American model. The US and the UK dominate its promotion and composition, although, as with all the models, there are inevitably important differences between countries within the bloc.

In contrast, other countries have a large basic, state-run, pay-as-you-go system, frequently with some earnings-related component. Some countries, such as Germany and France in particular, emphasise what they call 'solidarity between and within different generations', a sentiment which is absent from the Anglo-American bloc. Alongside the state-run system there may be either a relatively small supplementary scheme run by private financial institutions and invested on stock markets or a supplementary, pay-as-you-go system run by employers and employees. Alternatively, contributions may be credited to a corporate account without any 'investment' taking place or physical 'assets' being created. In essence, there is little 'funding'. This is the European model (again, with the variants).

Third, there are funded, but state-run, invested schemes, usually referred to as national or central provident funds. There may or may not be a 'basic'. Let us call this the Asian-Pacific model.

Finally there is everywhere else with a formal system, usually consisting wholly of a state, unfunded pension system – there are no 'investments' and no private sector to speak of. They can, or could, be found mainly in Central and Eastern Europe and other former Communist or CIS countries (the Commonwealth of Independent States, or some former members of the Soviet Union) – what I have called the Eurasian model.

Let us now consider the countries in the various blocs. Then we will look at the importance of the arguments in the context of world financial issues. After this we will consider the different welfare or pension systems in relation to finance and production systems. This will be followed by a more detailed examination of the case for privately funded provision and its consequences for markets and economic development.

THE WORLD'S WELFARE BLOCS

The Four Models of Provision

I have tried to summarise the different approaches to pensions as follows and to place the main countries in their appropriate groups. Again, there are many subtleties and differences within the various groups, as we shall see, but as a basic structure it provides us, at least initially, with the key issues for consideration.

1. Anglo-American (the US, the UK, the Netherlands, Ireland, Switzerland, Australia, Chile, South Africa, Canada and, more arguably, Japan).
2. European (the European Union, minus the UK, the Netherlands and Ireland, but plus Norway).
3. Asian-Pacific (Singapore, Malaysia, Sri Lanka, Fiji, along with smaller examples in certain countries in Africa, and in India and Indonesia).
4. Eurasian (former Communist countries, again with some similar structures elsewhere, including urban China).

Table 1 Dominant Pension Arrangements
Three Models of Pensions Provision
(Anglo-American, European, Asian-Pacific)

A. ANGLO-AMERICAN
'*Supplementary*', funded, *privately* invested is dominant
- pre-funding through savings invested on stock markets
- role of state minimised or viewed as a burden
- private financial institutions maximised
- reliance on the stock market
- only partial coverage
- small state *basic*, unfunded, universal coverage

B. EUROPEAN
'*Basic*' or state-run system out of current revenue is dominant
- no, or limited funding
- large role for the state
- no, or limited role for financial institutions
- mistrust of stock markets
- universal coverage
- small (in terms of invested assets), private *supplementary*, (i) funded or (ii) unfunded (but can be significant in terms of coverage)

C. ASIAN-PACIFIC
'*Supplementary*', funded or part funded, *publicly* invested is dominant or important
- pre-funding through state investment
- national or central 'provident funds'
- large investment in state securities
- extensive or universal coverage
- small state, unfunded *basic*, or none

Let us put to one side, for the time being, the Eurasian model (no. 4 above), since this is the extreme case of a public, non-funded system, with broad, universal coverage and no formal supplementary or private arrangements of any sort. It is a variant of the European model in certain respects. What I want to concentrate on is the relative weight and structure of private systems, and especially funded systems under private management.

Table 2 Country Statistics by Welfare Bloc

Country	Public expenditure on state pensions (% GDP) various years 1985–92	Supplementary pensions coverage (% labour force) various years 1989–96	Funded pension assets (% GDP) mostly 1996	GDP growth 1985–95 (average annual)
US	6.5	55	58.2	2.5
UK	9.5	75	74.7	2.3
Switzerland	9.9	100	117.1	1.6
Netherlands	9.8	82	87.3	2.6
Ireland	6.1	52	45.0	4.2
Australia	3.9	60	42.0	2.9
Chile	5.7	55*–86[†]	40.0	6.8
South Africa		70	57.0	1.0
Japan	5.0	38	41.8	3.1
Canada	4.2	45	43.0	2.2
Anglo-American average	*6.7*	*66*	*60.6*	*2.9*
Austria	14.8	10	1.2	2.6
Belgium	11.0	5	4.1	2.2
Denmark	9.9	80	23.9	1.7
France	11.8	90	5.8	2.2
Finland	10.3	0	10.0	1.0
Germany	10.8	46	5.8	2.8
Greece	12.3	5	12.7	1.4
Italy	14.4	5	3.0	2.0
Luxembourg	12.0	30	19.7	5.9
Portugal	7.7	15	9.9	3.2
Spain	7.5	15	3.8	2.9
Sweden	11.6	100	32.6	1.0
Norway	10.1	25	7.3	2.5
European average	*10.8*	*27*	*10.4*	*2.4*

Table 2   (Continued)

Country	Public expenditure on state pensions (% GDP) various years 1985–92	Supplementary pensions coverage (% labour force) various years 1989–96	Funded pension assets (% GDP) mostly 1996	GDP growth 1985–95 (average annual)
Singapore	2.2	90	73.0	8.2
Malaysia	1.6	49	40.8	7.6
Fiji	8.5		43.9	
Asian-Pacific average	*4.0*		*51.5*	*7.9*

Sources: World Bank, 1994; EFRP, 1996; OECD, 1998a; The Economist, *Pocket World in Figures*, London, 1998; and individual enquiries; *unofficial; †official.

The first two models outlined above portray different balances between the state and the private sector which have come to dominate current debates. The third shows that there are cases where the state controls investment. All three show different balances between the basic and the supplementary, and funding and non-funding (summarised in Tables 1 and 2 and Figure 1). This is not to ignore the fact that the main debate is between the Anglo-American model, with its variants, and everything else, as demonstrated by the World Bank (World Bank, 1994; James, 1996 – Estelle James was the leader of the team which produced the World Bank report).

The classification of countries in the list above and in Table 2 according to the various welfare blocs is based on the following considerations. Let us consider the blocs, taking them in the order outlined above.

1. Anglo-American. Private control and funded arrangements dominate – funding through a system of personal savings which are invested on stock markets via financial institutions. This means that people pay

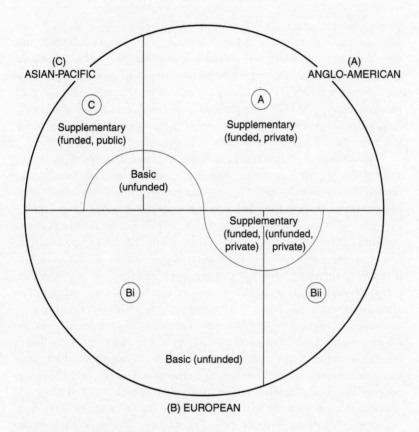

Figure 1 Dominant Pension Arrangements

for their own pensions by saving and investing, using banks, insurance companies and other fund managers to invest the savings on their behalf. This can be organised on an occupational (company), industry-wide or national and individual basis, and can be compulsory or not. I have classified this 'supplementary' system as 'dominant' where it covers around 40 per cent of the working population and where its assets (invested funds) are equivalent to 40 per cent of national GDP. I know that these percentages are rather arbitrary, but they appear to provide a reasonable guide to the overall structure given the difficulties, on which I want to comment below, of quantitative measurement. The basic pension is frequently flat-rate and minimal, but in the US state provision of pensions, or social security, has an earnings-related component and a significant element of redistribution from higher- to lower-income groups.

2. *European.* In this system the basic pension dominates pension arrangements, with a strong earnings-related element, run by the state – the so-called 'public pay-as-you-go' schemes. This means that pensions are paid as they fall due through compulsory state systems of social insurance, taxation and public expenditure; that is, current workers contribute in large part to the income of current pensioners. These are accompanied by supplementary pensions which can be significant in terms of coverage but are normally small or negligible in terms of assets. Either there is a private, funded scheme using insurance companies and other fund managers (Scandinavian countries), or there is a privately run pay-as-you-go system ('repartition') run by employers and employees (France), or there is the private 'book reserve' or 'direct commitment' system ('*Direktzusage*') in which pension contributions are attributed to corporate reserves, and there are no physical assets as such (Germany and Luxembourg). These will also often co-exist with insurance arrangements and, in Germany, some small pension funds (for France, see Reynaud, 1994; for Germany, see Steinmeyer, 1999). Other continental European countries have very small insurance- or pension-related funds sitting alongside a much more significant pay-as-you-go and earnings-related state scheme (for Italy, see Ascoli, 1996, and more generally on other European pension arrangements, ENRSP I – see notes for definition).

3. *Asian-Pacific.* The third model has a dominant publicly run investment scheme in addition to, sometimes, a very small basic scheme. The investment schemes are normally called provident funds and have

extensive or universal coverage. They can invest heavily in government securities. I classify these as dominant where, again, there is 40 per cent coverage (normally much higher) and assets are equivalent to 40 per cent of GDP (Singapore, Malaysia and Fiji). They are also important where there is 40 per cent coverage and assets equivalent to 10 per cent of GDP (Sri Lanka, Kenya, Barbados).

DIFFICULTIES IN QUANTITATIVE MEASUREMENTS OF WELFARE SYSTEMS

I want to discuss further the problems of measuring the different welfare systems and how I have tried to tackle some of the issues involved in quantitative assessments.

From the broader economic point of view, for instance, coverage by itself is not sufficient as a measure of the relative importance of different systems. Denmark has extensive coverage by a funded system (80 per cent of private-sector employment), but this is 'supplementary' to the tax-based, pay-as-you-go system, since the assets of the funded system (at least at the moment) amount to just over 20 per cent of GDP. In contrast, the UK has about 50 per cent coverage (by occupational pension arrangements, plus up to 25 per cent by personal pension plans) but the assets by the mid-1990s were equivalent to around 75 per cent of GDP.

Perhaps state expenditure on pensions is a better measure. In the UK this expenditure, at less than 10 per cent of UK GDP, is among the lowest in the European Union and the OECD, while the proportions of the population over sixty and over sixty-five in 1990 were higher than the average for the EU and OECD. In the US the proportions were lower than average but pensions expenditure was disproportionately lower, as was the case in Australia and Ireland.

However, direct state expenditure, in any case, can only be an indicative measure of public pensions policy. It omits non-cash receipts, such as housing, both public and private, as well as tax concessions, target groups and take-up groups. If non-cash receipts are included, for example, rankings remain the same – countries like Sweden and the Netherlands are still the most equal and the US the most unequal, with the highest proportion of older people with relatively low incomes – but some of the differences between countries are significantly narrowed (Whiteford and Kennedy, 1995, and for a longer discussion about the problems of quantifying welfare states, Esping-Andersen, 1990).

Richard Titmuss offered another very important and fascinating qualification to the measurement of welfare systems by domestic public expenditure. He introduced an international dimension. For example, the migration of doctors from other countries to the US after 1949, he argued at the time of his research, saved the country no less than $4 billion. This 'foreign aid' to the US was greater than the total of US foreign aid to other countries during this period, he maintained (Titmuss, 1976, p. 125). So, by implication, some countries were, in effect, subsidising others.

Most importantly, however, expenditure *per se*, however significant, says little about dynamics, which are naturally, or apparently, more subjective. In other words, it is not only that private pension fund assets have come to be an essential part of public assessments of the economic importance of different systems. Even more relevant, I would contend, is the apparent direction or intent of the system as implied by policy statements, legislative changes, the theoretical arguments used to justify policies and the general trends over time.

Thus, funded schemes are usually described as 'supplementary' in official terminology, as opposed to unfunded, 'basic' pensions. But, in my judgement, on the basis of policy statements and trends, along with their legislative and theoretical underpinning, the Anglo-American model seeks to reverse this in order to make supplementary schemes the dominant form of provision. Indeed, it aims to encourage private saving by reducing public provision.

In the UK, even the original Beveridge proposals of 1942 envisioned the state pension as solely providing enough for subsistence.

The Beveridge report stated, in the section on old age, that 'direct encouragement of voluntary insurance or saving to meet abnormal needs or to maintain standards of comfort above subsistence level, is an essential part of the Plan for Social Security proposed in this Report' (Beveridge, 1966 reprint, pp. 92–3). Future Labour government proposals to introduce a state earnings-related scheme were undermined by concurrent proposals to enable individuals to opt out of this into a private arrangement with favourable tax incentives.

Put another way, in the European model, supplementary schemes can be described, in general terms, as indeed *complementary*. In the Anglo-American model, the dynamics of policy-development suggest instead that they tend to be *substitutional* (comparative concepts which I draw from Ascoli, 1996). Policy-makers and their advisers increasingly want them to take on the importance of basic state systems.

ANGLO-AMERICAN MEMBERS IN EUROPE – WHY THE NETHERLANDS?

Given the historical importance of the stock market, it is relatively straightforward to understand the minimalist, liberal position towards the state advocated by the UK and, perhaps by association, Ireland. But why is the Netherlands the only country in continental (EU) Europe which has an Anglo-American pension system, as I have classified the systems?

One explanation is the cultural and social attitude to the state. This suggests that the state has no history of engagement in society and the economy comparable to the Scandinavian countries or Germany, Italy and France, where 'the state is by historical convention the most important and least-contested participant in the political arena' (Judt, 1997, p. 107). I am not so sure about this given the importance of the state in the Dutch mercantile system of the seventeenth and eighteenth centuries (Arrighi, 1994).

Perhaps an alternative explanation is this. In the UK and the

Netherlands, there has been a greater role for financial accumulation through stock markets and international trading companies than elsewhere in Europe. After the city-state of Genoa, the Netherlands (United Provinces), followed by the UK and the US, were the dominant centres of financial capitalism from the seventeenth century to the twentieth (as reviewed in Arrighi, 1994). Amsterdam was central to the development of 'merchant banking' itself, and could boast the world's first permanent stock exchange. Many individuals and families, such as the Barings family, originated in the Netherlands (see Chapman, 1984, for a history of merchant banking which also includes the contribution of Barings).

The jewel in the crown of the United Provinces' mercantilism, the Dutch East India Company, did not finally go bankrupt until 1799. But already by the beginning of the eighteenth century, Dutch financiers had moved to investing in the growth of the British imperial and financial system. This followed the relative decline in ascendancy of the Netherlands' own commercial regime. Britain had emerged as an alternative avenue for Dutch investment following Britain's commercial gains in the war of the Spanish succession at the turn of the eighteenth century.

By 1737 the Dutch held one-fifth of England's national debt and by 1758 they owned one-third of the Bank of England, the English East India Company and South Sea stocks (Arrighi, 1994, p. 207), revealing not for the first time, and certainly not the last, the lack of national sentiment of money. The Dutch financial dealings, or speculation, included getting in and out of the South Sea Bubble before it burst (Kindleberger, 1996, pp. 112 and 125).

Arguably, these factors have created a greater social and political legitimacy for the use of financial markets and international portfolio investment than can be found in other continental European countries. These other European countries have never featured as such significant centres of mercantile *and* financial trade. Thus we have a much larger stock market and a greater role for invested pension funds in the Netherlands than elsewhere.

OTHER ASPECTS OF THE SYSTEMS

One or two other observations need to be mentioned in the assessment of the direction and philosophy of the various systems.

Most pension schemes, to date, have been 'defined-benefit', whether basic or supplementary. That is, the pension is more or less known in advance, often also related to years of employment and contributions or citizenship. New supplementary, funded schemes are increasingly 'defined-contribution'. The benefit is not known but depends on contributions and, crucially, investment returns – 'money purchase' schemes (what you contribute plus investment returns are what you get) as opposed to 'final salary' schemes (defined benefit based on a salary-related formula).

Defined-contribution schemes are said, variously, to (a) increase labour mobility (contributors do not suffer from unfavourable 'transfer values' when changing employers, they carry their pension scheme and agreed contribution rate with them); (b) lower employment costs (there is no 'guarantee' from the employer); (c) increase choice (there is competition between a number of pension providers); and (d) lower pension costs to the consumer (the result of the competition between the providers).

This formula applies to personal pensions in the UK and the individual retirement funds in the US ('401[k] accounts'), as well as the pension plan in Chile. The World Bank views these arrangements as perhaps superior to the company-based, occupational, defined-benefit pension scheme model (although the pensions provision for the World Bank's own employees falls into the latter category and may indeed, through the overall generosity of labour benefits, ironically be seen to inhibit labour mobility).[1]

Turning to the geographical dimension, as opposed to the abstract systems and funding structures, there is a virtual encirclement of the globe by countries with what I have judged to be predominantly funded systems managed by private financial institutions – the Anglo-American model. As a crucial part of this, the importance of domestic financial markets is also growing – both the number of stock markets and their value are increasing rapidly, despite hiccups, as is the share of 'emerging markets' in world stock-market capitalisation (defined as total world share values, IFC, 1998), again despite some of the afore-mentioned hiccups.

Although there are many subtleties and differences in approaches, and, as we shall see, often resistance, the model is spreading down from North to South America, from the UK and the US to Central and Eastern Europe, and has a growing presence in the Pacific area. Some Scandinavian countries appear, from the figures, to be approaching a dominant private, funded model. In Sweden, even part of the basic state pension has been switched into investment in private mutual funds or premium pension accounts. I shall come back to the Scandinavian variants in more detail below. (See Figure 2.)

As is to be expected, when we consider the figures in Table 2, some may argue for a separate grouping, or at least a sub-grouping in the categories for certain countries. Australia, for example, is often seen as different from the mainstream funded model because of the very important role of trade unions. Trade unions were instrumental in extending private pension benefits to major parts of the workforce. The history of this is extremely important in understanding the politics and economics of funded arrangements in Australia. Furthermore, Ireland, another member of the Anglo-American group, according to my definition, has legislation which provides for pension boards to include 50 per cent of member-nominated trustees. Some also see similarities between Scandinavia (to lump together a group of countries which also have important differences in various respects) and Australia in the levels of funding and the role of 'labour'. In particular, in Denmark and Australia, the funded, or defined-contribution, systems have been underpinned by collective bargaining, with statutory support, while other countries, like the Chilean exemplar, have not. In the former case the results have reportedly included much lower costs and wider coverage.

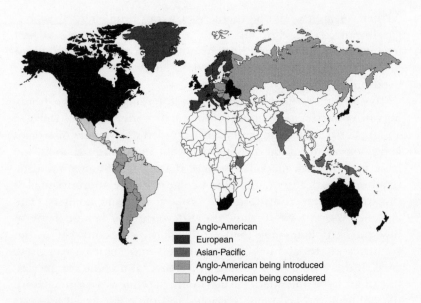

Figure 2　Map of the World's Welfare Blocs

The argument for a separate grouping based on the role of labour is challenging. But for the purpose of my thesis it fails to consider the stock market/investment side of the equation. I would contend that the overall thrust of funding, investment policy and stock markets in Australia is substantially different to the approach, generally speaking, in Scandinavian countries. In the Scandinavian countries, funding appears to be genuinely supplementary (complementary) with much higher levels of public expenditure underpinning the entire system, while in Australia the public system is residual. Scandinavian countries also do not have investment policies which are 'free' and 'open'. Their investment policies are, in the words of critics, frequently 'restricted'. In Denmark, for instance, pension funds receive no tax concessions for investment outside the domestic economy of Denmark itself. But further research would be useful. As Charles Kindleberger has elegantly put it in a different context, the argument here is 'not irrefutable' (Kindleberger, 1996, p. 192: he was discussing the role of 'lender of last resort' in financial crises, another influential actor in determining investment behaviour).

To sum up, there are certainly many differences within the groupings of countries contained within each model or bloc. Debates about classifications can, and have, occupied many pages of articles and books on the subject. But given what I have argued about the basic role of stock markets I believe that clear evidence would be required in order to modify what I believe are the appropriate classifications when considering a broad economic analysis. The evidence would have to show the difference that labour made to investment policies *and* to the role of the stock market in the countries where labour is said to play an important part in these areas. If there is no such evidence then there is no basis for my classifications to be amended. Furthermore, in so far as we can measure the political and economic variables and the commercial interests behind the models (which I shall spell out later), my prognosis is that the Anglo-American model will spread further. Of course, there are many factors which create inertia in systems, making them difficult to change, but at least the political arguments which support the Anglo-American model are increasing in importance and criticisms of the existing public arrangements have never been more frequent or comprehensive. The European model appears increasingly on the defensive.

In blunt commercial and political terms, as we shall see, the European and other non-Anglo-American models have no commercial forces driving them. They are generally based on some assumptions about the virtues of the role of the state and also frequently contain a different view of companies themselves – more as social institutions than sources of 'shareholder value' for pension fund investment. But despite some attempts by Western European countries to transfer their experience to Central and Eastern European countries engaged in social and economic 'reform', in the last resort the former simply have nothing to 'sell'.

THE DIVIDE BETWEEN THE MODELS

Let us now restate the fundamental difference between the approaches to pensions provision.

The European model uses phrases like 'solidarity between different generations' in its self-description (CEC, 1997). Whatever the reality of the claim, it reflects an important element in the philosophy of pay-as-you-go systems, which aim, in principle, to redistribute out of current income to current pensioners. We shall examine the intergenerational issue in more detail in a later chapter.

But the issue is not just whether pension systems are, or should be, funded or pay-as-you-go, or some combination of the two, or public or private or, again, some mixture of the two. Public schemes can be funded, and private schemes can be pay-as-you-go, defined-benefit or defined-contribution. There are multiple combinations and there is much literature describing and recommending various arrangements which claim to produce the best benefits according to local circumstances. The issue is also not really about quantifiable differences in expenditure, however defined and quantified. My argument is that *the clear pensions divide is between those systems that use private financial institutions and relatively 'unrestricted' private markets, and which argue for the 'free movement of capital', and those that do not.* The issue is thus quite simple. It should not be obscured by arguments which fail to address the fundamental point about the nature of the welfare/finance/production system which underlies some of the seemingly obscure technical points.

To explain this more fully we must go back to the optimism about welfare and the regulation of financial systems at the end of the Second World War. Our discussions will sometimes take us back even earlier. The point is to examine how private pensions have become a crucial part of financial systems and the enormous flows of private funds, nationally and internationally. This will help us to understand what is really at stake when we consider the world's welfare divisions and the arguments for one kind of pension system or another. It will also set the context for an examination of the real implications for production, investment and broader social welfare.

2

Financial Markets and
Pension Funds

First, I need briefly to reiterate a few relatively well known facts and arguments about the development of the current international financial system. Then we can place pension funds in the operation of this system and assess their importance, a less well rehearsed undertaking.

THE POST-SECOND WORLD WAR FINANCIAL SYSTEM

As we know, the Bretton Woods agreement in 1944 established the World Bank and the IMF – the 'Bretton Woods institutions' – along with a monetary system which influenced the world economy for many years. Currency adjustments based on a country's balance of payments were kept within limits, supported by short-term credits to aid adjustment from the IMF. The US dollar underpinned the system. The Communist bloc was not a part of the arrangements. The World Bank and the IMF remain, but their roles have changed, as we have seen particularly in the many reports and debates about them following the world financial crises which started in 1997.

To cut a now familiar and long story short, exchange rates based on parities with the US dollar and, ultimately, gold were abandoned in favour of floating rates in 1973. The cost of the war in Vietnam was a significant factor which led the US to withdraw from its key role in the international monetary system. Controls on capital movements, a key part of the 'Bretton Woods' system, were subsequently abandoned.

The system was already under considerable strain. 'Euromarkets' had started their inexorable rise in the 1950s, initially a trade in dollars outside the currency controls of the US, instigated by the Communist governments of China and the Soviet Union, who were trying to keep their dollars outside of US jurisdiction. But they were not the deciding factor. There was, first, a major expansion of US corporate capital into Europe in the 1950s and 1960s. This followed on from the Marshall Plan for European reconstruction, which was prompted by the per-ceived Communist threat to Europe and elsewhere, especially after the Korean conflict. Next, the early 1970s witnessed a further surge of dollars into Europe as a result of President Nixon's loosening of US monetary policy in his 1971–72 re-election bid. This occurred at the time when the Deutsche Bundesbank was tightening interest rates to combat inflation (Kindleberger, 1996, p. 19). So dollars fled to Europe to earn higher rates of interest.

In any event, what began as an 'offshore' dollar market (trade in dollar-denominated securities outside US controls), with London the chief location for the offshore centre, soon became a market in many other currencies. These markets were subsequently enhanced by the flows of 'petrodollars' resulting from the oil price increases of the mid-1970s. Currency controls had started to weaken with the specula-tion against the pound sterling in the 1960s, leading to its devaluation in 1967. Despite attempts at international agreements and 'Accords' from the 1970s onwards, exchange rates, interest rates, debt levels, inflation and public expenditure became far more susceptible to the flows of finance in the international financial markets.

These markets dwarf the currency reserves of individual countries, with the IMF now providing rescue packages, or 'bail-outs', designed to restore 'confidence' to the financial markets. Its new role started with the Latin American debt crisis (which was fuelled by Nixon's monetary policy, which pushed money into anything promising higher returns). This role was then extended to Russia and Eastern Europe after the collapse of the Communist bloc, and then to South-east Asia and Korea after the 1997 currency crises.

Most importantly for our analysis, however, the question is this: what is the role of pensions in this historical excursion?

THE ROLE OF PENSIONS

After Eurodollars and petrodollars came 'pension dollars'. They began their enormous growth in the 1970s, coinciding with the end of the post-war economic agreement and the rapid expansion of the new financial flows and markets. They were often seen as ways of 'deferring' wages in the 'stagflation' period following the post-Second World War, so-called 'Golden Age' of growth which ended with the abandonment of the Bretton Woods agreements. This was followed by the 'Leaden Age' – for some at least, but not for pension funds.

The OECD puts the figure for total pension assets at $8.7 trillion (thousand billion) for the OECD countries for 1996 – an annual average growth rate of 10.9 per cent since 1990 (OECD, 1998b). It estimates that pension funds comprise 28 per cent of all institutional finance in the OECD (this includes insurance companies, investment companies, pension funds and others for 1995).

Table 3 shows the growth rates for the financial assets of these institutions and it reveals the relative significance of pension funds. But these figures for pension funds, taken by themselves, underestimate the importance of pension-related institutional activity. They exclude the pension-related activity of insurance companies, which is included in the insurance figures (mainly in the UK) and mutual funds (in the US), alongside other similar institutions elsewhere in the OECD. Their inclusion in the figures concerning pensions would probably increase the figure to nearer $10,000 billion, or over 40 per cent of the OECD total, for pension-related investment assets. The addition of non-OECD countries would increase the absolute monetary amount again.

Although the figures move around somewhat, and, according to my

Table 3   Average Annual Rate of Growth of Assets Held by Institutional
Investors in OECD Regions, 1990–95 (%)

	Europe (20 countries)	North America	Asia and Pacific
Insurance companies	11.4	7.9	9.2
Pension funds	6.8	10.1	11.1
Investment companies	16.5	18.7	7.6
All	11.3	10.9	8.3

Source: adapted from OECD, 1998a, p. 30.

discussions with the OECD, appear to be rather dependent on individual countries' estimations, I estimate that the total for worldwide
pension assets is over $12,000 billion for the end of the 1990s and the
beginning of the new millennium.

In contrast, US GDP for 1998 was $7,000 billion; the GDP of
countries in the Anglo-American bloc was $14,000 billion. Total
world stock-market capitalisation for 1997 was $23,000 billion and
total world GDP for 1998 was $28,000 billion. So we have a possible
$12,000 billion of global pension fund assets versus a world GDP of
only two to two and a third times that much. Pension funds are
indeed significant. I am not confusing stocks (assets) and flows (GDP,
a recurring item) but trying to give measures of relative size. But
there *is* a relationship.

Thus, global pension fund assets amount to nearly 43 per cent of
world GDP. The relationship between the two is this. The (growing)
pension fund 'stock' has an increasing, if not crucial, influence on the
'flows' of world GDP. The relationship between the two, and whether
the former represents realistic claims on the latter, as we shall see
later, is central to some of the arguments and counter-arguments
about the real 'value' of pension funds and the attendant theory of
economic growth.

Let us step back from the crucial arguments for a moment in order to provide some other measures of comparative size and potential influence. Private pension funds and pension-related systems are invested on stock markets and now form a significant part of world financial markets. Pension fund assets alone amount to over ten times the size of all the foreign currency reserves of the fifteen largest 'Western' economies (most of the EU plus the US, Australia, Canada, Japan, Switzerland). In the US and the UK they own over 30 per cent of their respective stock markets (the market capitalisation of the companies quoted on those markets) and they are the largest institutional holders of company shares. They are followed in the UK by insurance companies and in the US by the mutual funds, both of whose official statistics, as mentioned above, include personal pensions money (for example, 15–20 per cent of the $35,000 billion retail US fund-management business in 1996).

Pension funds and their assets are controlled by international financial institutions, such as banks and insurance companies. These companies manage other capital and perform other financial functions, such as advice and management services to governments and companies nationally and internationally concerning fund-raising, privatisation and economic policy (Table 4). They have grown with the Eurodollars and petrodollars and the rise in international banking and investment, the growing takeover and privatisation business, as well as the domestic savings business. By 1998, the US and the UK were recorded as the largest exporters of services. The biggest element of these were business services, in particular activities involved in mergers and acquisitions, corporate finance and related activities.

The growth in the supply of funds has been accompanied by a continuous process of corporate concentration through merger and acquisition within the financial sector itself. By 1995, the world's top ten privately owned money-managers included mutual funds, insurance companies and banks, four from the US, three from Switzerland, one each from Japan and France (the newcomer) and one joint

Table 4 Financial Advisers: Functions and Services

Personal savings schemes and personal loans	Investment of individuals' accounts, premiums or personal pensions in shares and government securities; personal loans
Pension funds of public and private companies and authorities	Buying and selling shares, underwriting new issues and rights issues, investment in government debt
Privatising government-owned companies	Advice to governments and placing or underwriting the share issues
Mergers and acquisitions (M&A)	Advice to companies, placing or underwriting
New issues and rights issues	Advice to companies entering the stock market, and existing companies issuing shares; placing and underwriting
Loans to companies	Advice to companies and lending as secured creditors; loans for M&A
Loans to government	Advice to governments and lending so-called 'sovereign debt'

US/UK venture. They managed $3,600 billion of funds, including pension money. The foreign currency reserves of the US, the UK, Japan and Switzerland together amounted to one-tenth of this. Four years later, a survey by William Mercer, benefit consultants, examined a recent wave of takeover and merger activity in the financial sector. The consultants estimated that the top five groups of money-managers looked after assets of equivalent value to the combined GDP of the UK and France, while the top thirty-five managed $8,200 billion, rivalling the size of the US GDP (*Financial Times*, 1999a, p. 3).

This demonstrates the importance of pension funds in terms of volume and concentration of control. It also places pensions in the context of the financial markets as a whole. But what about the implications for the international monetary system and the flows of pension finance between countries? As we shall examine in more detail in a later chapter, this is an important part of the link between financial and welfare systems.

INTERNATIONAL PENSION FLOWS

The cross-border nature of these funds reveals the internationalisation of pension financial flows. Although various sources provide different figures, it can be reasonably concluded that, in total, over 12 per cent of *all* pension fund assets are invested outside their country of origin. In G-10 countries the figure is 17 per cent. The UK and the Netherlands are in the lead among the countries with large pension funds. They have around 30 per cent invested outside their home countries. Australia has 24 per cent. These investments, incidentally, also include bonds issued by the World Bank, the largest borrower on international capital markets.

The private capital is not for the most part 'direct investment' – the provision of finance for new capital investment in infrastructure, production or services or the promotion of productive investment in companies outside the domestic economy. It is mainly a trade in existing stocks and securities – the 'portfolio' markets of secondary stocks, shares and associated currencies, along with the purchase of newly issued stock, especially newly privatised companies.

In any case, foreign direct investment (FDI) is said to be smaller as a proportion of world output than before the First World War, whereas gross international financial flows are much bigger and have recently increased exponentially. Cross-border sales and purchases of bonds and equities by US investors have risen from the equivalent of 9 per cent of GDP in 1980 to 164 per cent in 1996. Currency trades in London, New York and Tokyo rose from $190 billion *a day* in 1985 to $1,200 billion in 1995.

Current-account balance of payments deficits can be a basis for funding growth – the deficit is balanced by borrowing money on the capital account from other countries to compensate for the lack of domestic capital. This happened in nineteenth-century America, Russia and the Far East for investment in railways and other infrastructure, and to some extent in Third World bank borrowing of the 1970s. The important point is the *nature* of international capital flows. Whether FDI, bank loans, bonds, equity issues or portfolio investment, the question is how much of it is 'flight capital' – funds that are not tied into specific investment projects – and how much is accounted for by pension funds. This then tells us something important about the implications of the Anglo-American stock market theory of welfare.

Flight capital, as opposed to long-term fixed capital or dedicated investment, is an essential part of the increase in capital mobility and the ending of capital controls. For instance, flight capital amounted to one-third of Latin America's external financing by 1992 (Cordery, 1994). Other countries and regions, whether 'developed', 'developing' or 'in transition', are increasingly affected by flight capital. The problem is to measure their significance and, for our purposes, to assess the role of pension investment.

Official statistics show that from 1994–97 only 3–5 per cent of international capital-market activity was equity investment, while 27–33 per cent took the form of bonds – tradable or 'securitised' loans with interest (OECD, 1997). Although pension funds are involved in bonds (up to 30 per cent of pension assets in the Netherlands), their main international assets are equities. But the equity investment referred to in official figures concentrates on equity *issues* (new equity capital, especially, for instance, privatisation programmes in developing economies). But we should take into account equities more generally (portfolio stocks or the trading in existing shares, not just new issues).

I estimate, from extrapolations of net investment flows and predictions of the growth in the international asset holdings of pension funds, that the international holdings of shares by pension funds are up to three times the official figures for new equity issues alone, and therefore their participation in international capital-market activity is considerably larger than previously thought. I shall return to the specific issue of emerging markets and pension fund investment.

Excessive Third World lending by Western banks created its own problems of repayment. Corporate investment and lending to governments has also been subject to defaults caused by changes in regime or inability to repay. But, as we shall see in more detail later, flight capital is 'liquid' investment and protects against the risks of non-payment and default by being able to withdraw at short notice (or so it hopes), creating financial 'shocks' with enormous knock-on effects for other countries, markets and asset values, as the rush for cash or some other haven commences in a subsequent panic. Again, this is another point which we shall examine in more detail further on, in this case when we look at financial crises and the role of pension funds.

SOCIAL SECURITY CAPITAL

Thus, the size of global financial flows is unprecedented and they are increasingly unpredictable in their activities. The crucial point is that they are now augmented by the way we pay for our retirement. They no longer depend on Communist governments and their Eurodollars, no longer on corporate bodies, banks and the world's oil-producers to supply the cash. They instead rely substantially on the structure of social security provision. I suggest that nothing of this nature, scale and geographical reach has happened before.[2]

This is certainly not to fall into the 'globalisation' mire, whereby everything is supposed to be becoming standardised, or whatever. The arguments for this variously suggest a new era of 'globalised' communications and money markets, an unprecedented enormity of economic trade and financial transfers, an unheard-of speed of global decision-making, stunning technological advances in communications and much else besides.

There is some apparent truth in the claims in terms of how we experience events in our daily lives. But the concept of globalisation is often presented as some neutral, 'post-industrial', 'post-modern' development, the like of which we have never seen before. It appears to be caused by inexplicable events which we do not really understand, but which appear to be part of the logical progression of technology and the 'free market' – some neutral, universalising 'revolution' in technology, culture and communications, supposedly abolishing national boundaries, separate identities and government powers. It appears deservedly to elevate the world's financial markets to the role of arbiters of national policies, at last finally uniting us all, post-Communism, in a non-ideological common approach to economic policy, consumption, democracy and the role of the market and the state.

Maybe there is some merit in considering whether 'Americanisation', or even 'Anglo-Americanisation', is a better way of describing at least some of these developments. This is certainly relevant to pension funds and, by implication, to a considerable extent, the importance of capital-market financial flows. In other words, there is not an independent spirit of 'globalisation' at work, finally free from ideological conflicts and able to liberate us all. Instead, there is a worldwide application of a particular approach to the structure of markets and welfare – what might be better and more provocatively described as Americanisation. In this approach, private finance is a part of economic strategies which clearly favour countries such as the US and the UK (the latter being the subsidiary partner in the corporate relationship). These two countries in particular have the financial institutions to exploit the potential for private institutional investment along with associated business services in corporate finance, privatisation, mergers and acquisition, and other financial aspects of the comprehensive Anglo-American model of finance and social security. I return to this hypothesis about Americanisation at the end of the book.

My point is that, whatever the history of financial empires, manias, investment, money markets and so on (Arrighi, 1994, Kindleberger, 1996), something rather novel has occurred which few writers take into account. In the world of what I have perhaps melodramatically characterised as competing welfare blocs, international financial flows do not emanate solely from the financial transfers arising from trade or corporate surpluses. Financial flows also spring from how we pay for the maintenance of a large and growing proportion of the population as defined by a certain stage in life. Indeed, the role of pension funds suggests a new paradigm of economic analysis whereby 'social' provision through flows of finance for income security has augmented international financial flows. 'Social security capital' is now as important as other sources of capital, if not more so as more and more people are encouraged in one way or another to save privately for their retirement. It is a key element in fuelling the expansion of financial markets. Also, economic reform policies increasingly rely on the expansion of private pension funds to help pay for the reform process.

Furthermore, this suggests a new approach to the study of financial capital. No longer does financial capital, or the financial sector, or the institutional investment system – however we describe the accumulation of money and its usage – arise from the expected sources. These conventional sources included corporate surpluses; companies switching into financial capital for more profitable uses; banks lending money and receiving returns and deposits; governments raising and lending money; private individuals and corporations holding investments on stock markets or putting their private savings into banks and savings institutions for 'a rainy day'. Instead, the nature of financial capital, as an identifiable private structure of investment and lending capacity, along with its relationship to the productive economy, is increasingly dependent on the structure of national welfare systems and the transfer of funds from the public administration to private fund managers. This is assisted by public subsidy and the rundown of state provision in favour of mandatory or publicly encouraged private provision.

Let us now look at some of the general differences between the systems of finance, production and welfare. This will help us to see the connections between the analyses of the different systems, although these analyses have usually addressed the subject matter from separate disciplinary points of view. Our examination of the politics and economics of pension funds on the one hand and finance/production systems on the other tries to bring together these different perspectives.

3

Typologies of Capitalism and
Welfare Systems

The next argument to consider, therefore, is this. As a result of the foregoing, my analysis of pension systems has implications for the analysis of 'capitalism' more generally.

Table 5 displays a number of ways of classifying the different systems of production and welfare. These classifications have appeared in literature on the two subjects. Some classifications are used in everyday discussions and are not clearly structured, but they often give an interesting popular view of current events, which can be as perceptive and interesting as theoretical analysis.

THE TWO AREAS OF CLASSIFICATION:
PRODUCTION/FINANCE AND WELFARE/
SOCIAL SECURITY

Essentially, all the classifications refer to either financial and production systems or welfare/social security systems, each considered separately from each other. There are many similarities in the approaches, and there are some common themes linking the philosophies of finance/production systems with their corresponding welfare systems, but there is little structural overlap between analyses of welfare/pension systems and finance/production systems in the

Table 5 Classifications of Welfare and Financial Systems

Welfare, Finance/Production	*Type 1* US/UK	*Type 2* Continental Europe	*Type 3* South-east Asia	*Type 4* Communist Bloc (current and ex), 'socialist' or ideal type
Welfare blocs	Anglo-American – use of financial markets	European – limited use of financial markets	Asian-Pacific – state-run investment funds	Eurasian
Welfare capitalisms	Liberal; means-testing and use of market	Corporatist-statist/social democratic-Scandinavian	(not specified)	Inclusive, 'non-commodifying' (Scandinavian nearest approximation)
Welfare states	Residual	Industrial achievement-performance	(not specified)	'Institutional redistributive' – universalist, non-market (Scandinavian nearest approximation)
Welfare regimes	Liberal (Protestant-liberal) US and Australia (inequality)	Conservative (Christian Democratic) Germany and France (status differentials)	Late female mobilisation; Japan and Spain (status differentials)	Social democratic (Protestant social democratic) Sweden and Denmark (redistributive) State bureaucratic collectivism (proletarianised with privileges)
Welfare states – two dimensions for *quantity* of coverage and *how* covered	Low social expenditure/low contributions versus tax (UK, Ireland)	High social expenditure, high contributions versus tax (Benelux, France, Germany)		High social expenditure, low contributions versus tax (Scandinavia)

		Low social expenditure high contributions (S. Europe, Switzerland)		
Welfare systems	Beveridge safety net – prevention of poverty	Bismarck social insurance – income maintenance	Provident funds with little redistribution	Social democratic tax- and citizenship-based
Positive–negative philosophy	Welfare is a burden	Welfare is part of working entitlement/ wage-based insurance	Welfare is economic investment	Welfare is right of citizenship
Financial systems	Capital-market-based	Bank-based and credit-based	Bank-based; credit-based with government intervention	Public ownership or control
Financial (bank and equity market) corporate business relationships	Arms-length	Interlocking banks and companies	Bank/firm/state with industrial policy	Command economy; market relations not important
Developed and developing capitalisms and markets	Atlantic capital	Rhine capital	Tiger economies (to 1997), emerging markets	Transition economies emerging markets (former Communism)
Debt to equity capital – reliance on banks rather than stock market	Low corporate debt/equity	High debt/equity	High debt/equity	State banks/public ownership, now growing stock markets and problematic banks
Role of savings and investment in production	Savings create investment	Investment creates savings	Profitability creates investment, creates savings	Not relevant historically

Table 5 (Continued)

Welfare, Finance/Production	Type 1 US/UK	Type 2 Continental Europe	Type 3 South-east Asia	Type 4 Communist Bloc (current and ex), 'socialist' or ideal type
Characterisations of finance/ production	Money-manager capitalism	Finance capital	Chaebol capitalism	Oligarchic capitalism (1990s, post-Communist countries)
Criticism of capitalisms	Casino capitalism	Bankers' capitalism	Crony capitalism	Bandit or hyena capitalism (former Communist countries)

Sources: row 1 is from this book; row 2, Esping-Andersen, 1990; row 3, Titmuss, 1974 and 1976; row 4, Deacon et al., 1997; row 5, Bonoli, 1997; row 9, Zysman, 1983, and Grabel, 1997. Also, Rybczynski, 1988; Minsky, 1989, and others on finance and production. Some rows summarise certain arguments found in different sources.

The total of the comments in each row or column do not necessarily add up to any individual commentator's or any theoretical position. I have also taken some liberties in the summaries and classifications, and I am aware that not everything 'fits' the title of a column.

As implied in the table, some see a clear difference between the Scandinavian system and the rest of Continental Europe (see especially Esping-Andersen 1990 and 1996). One interesting classification – from a Scandinavian viewpoint – groups the systems as threefold (note, in passing, the importance given to the role of women in this perspective):

- Scandinavia (Denmark, Sweden, Norway, Finland): social benefits for all citizens; extensive redistribution; diverse public sector; universal waged work for women;
- Corporatism (Continental Europe): social security based on breadwinner's position in labour market; majority of services private; waged work for women not widespread;
- Liberalism (US and UK): individual's position in the labour market crucial; redistribution limited; public services not developed.

(Finland: A Cultural Encyclopaedia, Finnish Literary Society, Helsinki, 1997)

Again, welfare systems are considered separately from the organisation of the different capitalist production and financial systems – although there are some apparent implications.

The feminist perspective is given full attention and analysis in Siaroff, 1994. This dimension is included in the Deacon summary described in the table.

conventional classifications. However, in the current debates about pensions, the typologies of finance/production welfare/social security should be considered together. This is for the following reasons, some of which we have already touched on.

Improved pensions are said to be dependent on private savings and investment, which must function through capital markets. Private savings and investment and the corresponding development of stock markets are also said to be crucial for production. 'Burdens' of public pensions, however, are alleged to be undermining production, competition and the expansion of the financial markets. The nature and extent of the private financial system moves to centre stage in the assessment of the sustainability of both the productive and welfare systems. The nature of the financial system becomes the common link between the two.

There has been a creeping recognition of the links between the two, but rarely can we find an analysis which links them together in a structured way. The debates about the relationship between finance and industry have gone on for years. The debates about welfare, social security and public or private solutions have also preoccupied different disciplines and have been subjects of debate for decades. Now the two fields of debate must be considered together. In particular, therefore, we have to examine the centrality of the financial system to both the productive *and* social redistribution sides of the economic equation.

A look at the history of these analyses is interesting in that it shows how the two subject matters have sometimes flirted with each other, but have never really become engaged. Zysman (1983) contrasts three types of financial system. First, there is the capital-market-based system – an arm's-length relationship between government and industry (the US, and probably the categorisation that comes nearest to our Anglo-American model). Second, Zysman describes a credit-based system with government intervention in various industrial processes or decisions (Japan and France). Third, there is a credit-based system dominated by financial institutions, whose market power gives them influence over industry and which is part of a 'negotiated style' of modern capitalism (Germany). This type of analysis concentrates on the finance/production relationship, and the role of government. The nature and/or influence of the welfare/social security system, though implied in the references to the financial institutions, is not considered to be very important.

Rybczynski (1988) moves a step further. In this more historical approach there is first the 'bank-oriented' system providing loans along with the owner-control of enterprises. Next, there is the 'market-oriented' system, with its capital markets and the separation of ownership and control along with the increasing importance of house-hold savings. Last, we have the 'securitised' system, with the rise of institutional investors, *including pension funds*.

Minsky (1989) describes a corporate capitalism of self-perpetuating corporate bureaucracies which are not beholden to financial markets, and where stockholders are individuals, not institutions. This system has significant welfare states, trade unions and transfer payments. But then comes 'money-manager capitalism' to replace it, prompted by the rise of *pension funds*, mutual funds and insurance companies. This stage of capitalism is characterised by a structure of professional managers who aim for the maximisation of short-term returns. Minsky also contrasts the returns from 'enterprise' with those from 'speculation', as differentiated by Keynes. The former are dividends, interest and retained earnings which are usefully invested. The latter are asset appreciations not resulting from investment of retained earnings. The managed money is the speculative capital of this stage of capitalism. It emphasises the value of financial assets, in particular ordinary shares.

Most recently Dore et al. (1999) discuss the varieties of capitalism in the twentieth century and they produce interesting summaries and comprehensive references. They conclude by discussing the prospects for convergence between the different systems and the possibility of changes in pension arrangements in the non-'Anglo-Saxon' models of capitalism, as they characterise them.

From some of the literature we start to get a flavour of the growing recognition of the influence of pension funds, and financial institutions more generally, in the process of financial accumulation and its relationship to the process of production. But the emphasis is on the finance/production relationship. We cannot understand from these analyses *why* pension funds – a welfare or social security phenomenon – have arisen and how they are possibly crucial for the system of finance and production. We cannot understand how their sustainability and growth have become central to the financial system, nor how the nature of the financial system has become central to the structure of the pension system. Indeed, this was not the purpose of these analyses.

For instance, authors describe the different finance/production systems and acknowledge the rise of pension funds as part of this. But they say nothing explicitly about the persistence of corporate/credit or bank-based financial systems alongside unfunded pension arrangements. In other words, they do not explain why there is an apparent correlation between bank-related financial systems and unfunded pension arrangements on the one hand and stock-market-based financial systems and funded pension arrangements on the other.

Thus, we still need to understand the reasons for the rise of pension funds, taking into account the structure of the financial system. We also need to understand more fully the process of mutual reinforcement in which the financial system affects the nature of the welfare system, and the welfare system the nature of the financial system. Further, how does this burgeoning money-market approach to welfare/social security at the same time affect investment in production? What is the circle of welfare-finance-production? Where does it start, and which way round does it go?

Of course, in the literature there is inevitably some cross-reference between the separate typologies of finance/production and welfare/social security. Historically, there have been continual, albeit implicit, links between analyses of welfare problems and social requirements on the one hand, and the needs of production on the other.

John Grahl and Paul Teague (1997), for example, portray the European social model as a specific combination of comprehensive welfare systems and strongly institutionalised and politicised forms of industrial relations. Every aspect of the economic situation of the population can be an object of social policy and nearly every country rejects the legitimacy of purely market outcomes in the social sphere. The two authors note a certain level of convergence between employment and social security systems and the American model as a result of changes in industrial requirements – moves towards decentralised bargaining, 'flexible' employment patterns, sub-contracting, self-employment and so on. The links between welfare and production are apparent (see also Gough, 1996; Esping-Andersen, 1996).

However, to stress the main point again, my argument is that *the nature of the financial system, and its relationship to both production and welfare, has become central to the dynamic of the whole structure. That dynamic, which unites the whole economic and social system, prioritises the concept of the stock market as the arbiter of (a) the control and pricing of companies – the production relationship – and (b) the returns obtainable from stock-market dealings for pension payments – the welfare/social security relationship.*

The work of Minsky and others, to whom I have referred, certainly begins to outline some of these relationships, showing how pension arrangements have contributed to different structures of economic management. But in the other camp, unfortunately, authors who compare welfare/social security systems usually say nothing about the financial system or even, in many cases, private pension arrangements. They concentrate on state systems of welfare/pensions as if they are isolated in some 'black box' of the politics of social redistribution. Although these analyses are not always inconsistent with the classifications that I have tried to give, differences arise because the role of private provision is ignored. As I have tried to argue, the nature of the state system cannot be discussed independently of the role of private provision.

To take one example, to which I have referred in Table 5, in an interesting analysis Giulano Bonoli compares European countries in a two-pronged approach in terms of public expenditure. He uses, first, the percentage of GDP represented by social expenditure, and second, the percentage of social expenditure financed by contributions – the latter variable aimed at measuring the difference between Bismarck-type (social insurance) systems and Beveridge-type (to some extent, non-contribution-based) systems. He ends up with four groupings. One includes four Scandinavian countries, another the UK and Ireland; but, in a third, Switzerland is grouped with Italy, Spain, Greece and Portugal, and in a fourth the Netherlands is grouped with Belgium, Germany, France and Luxembourg (Bonoli, 1997).

Based on my own criteria for classifications, I would therefore argue that these groupings are inadequate for analysing pension systems, because they totally ignore private arrangements and their financial and economic implications. This demonstrates how a concentration on the state system alone is not sufficient.

In a more recent publication, Robert Goodin and colleagues compare social security in the US, Germany and the Netherlands. They conclude that the 'social democratic' regime represented, in their analysis, by the Netherlands is superior in terms of the moral objectives of welfare arrangements to the 'liberal' US regime and the 'corporatist' German model (Goodin et al., 1999). In fact, they maintain that the Netherlands presents a better exemplar of the social democratic model than Sweden itself – the country which is normally assumed to be the leader in the social democratic welfare regime. But private pension arrangements through stock markets are ignored. This in my view produces a substantial modification to the criteria to be used – whether moral, economic or political – and leads to a completely different classification for, among others, the Netherlands. The Netherlands basic pension is also flat-rate and not earnings-related, and in the second half of the 1990s there were government proposals to cut costs further.

Goodin and co-authors also very usefully refer to the plethora of work on welfare and social security classifications, showing how each new analysis introduces a 'novel twist' in the criteria and arguments in order to establish some claim to fame. Most, however, essentially support the basic classifications recorded by Richard Titmuss and Gøsta Esping-Andersen some time ago, with some subsequent modifications.

My 'novel twist' concerns the importance of the private sector and the role of stock markets. I also maintain, by implication, that we need to include the nature of the finance/production system in the comparison of welfare/social security systems. This will demonstrate the economic and social importance of both public and privately organised arrangements in the overall structure of welfare provision. The reason is, as I have stated, that the pensions and financial systems are intrinsically linked. This link is also important now that pensions comprise such a significant part of public expenditure on welfare and now that private arrangements have a significant and increasing role in total pensions provision. Concentrating on just the welfare system, public *and* private, is not sufficient if we exclude a parallel analysis of the financial system and the links between the two. Conversely it would be almost impossible now to discuss the finance/production system of money-managers by ignoring the role of private pension funds.

EXTERNAL DETERMINANTS

Previous criteria for classifying and explaining welfare systems have concentrated on factors such as the extent of industrialisation, the degree of working-class mobilisation, the influence of organised labour and social democratic parties, the self-interest of the state, social control and other associated variables (for example, Williamson and Pampel, 1993). All these factors are *internal* to a particular nation state.

Now, not only is the link between financial systems and welfare an essential internal part of the structures, but we also have an additional *external* factor to consider – the influence on governments and welfare systems of the financial markets and stock markets themselves in determining or influencing the nature of the welfare (pensions/ social security) system and, as we shall see, of the production system too.

Adam Harmes has discussed the structural power of institutional investors and their bias against stimulative macroeconomic policies (Harmes, 1998). Their tendency to 'overshoot' or over-react to economic circumstances, or so-called economic fundamentals and currency movements, in my view exerts a certain pressure on levels of public expenditure as a result of their views about the most appropriate policies for controlling inflation.

There has been an interesting parallel development in research concerning external factors. Bob Deacon and colleagues have examined the role of international agencies such as the World Bank, the European Union, the International Labour Office (ILO), the IMF and the United Nations in the development of social policy. Their work describes the different policy preferences of these agencies and the divisions between and within them in their promotion of welfare models throughout the world (Deacon et al., 1997). We shall indeed come across these policies and differences again in later chapters.

These international agencies are clearly a significant external factor in national social policy-development. My argument about pension funds and the financial markets, however, is that these agencies and markets, on balance, reinforce one particular model of welfare which is being propagated and implemented by private financial institutions and markets themselves, along with companies, governments and trade unions. There are, of course, differences within and between the international agencies and their policies, but the balance of advantage seems to favour one particular model of capitalist structures – what I have called the Anglo-American model. I shall return to explanations of why I consider this to be the case when I discuss the various domestic and non-domestic reasons for the adoption of the Anglo-American model or its variants.

THE CENTRALITY OF THE EQUITY MARKET

Looking down the columns in Table 5 it is possible to make links between welfare and finance/production classifications. The common thread weaving its way throughout is indeed the capital market. This, I would argue, has strong explanatory power when we examine the typologies of welfare and finance/production systems. Where there is a capital-market approach to welfare in which the role of the state is residual or the role of private investment markets is widely held out as an important supplement or replacement, the emphasis on the capital market as a means of financing production or, more realistically in practice, of determining the ownership and control of enterprises is greater.

In fact the two dimensions have come together. The *equity market* is central to both. This has even turned the intuitive logic of production, finance and social distribution on its head – reversing the cycle of private profit and social benefits. For instance, we think of productive investment as the motor for financing social distribution through the creation of profit, followed by state intervention through taxation or the regulation of employment conditions to enhance social welfare, as generally understood. Instead we now have a proposition in which the pension system is seen as foremost, or at least significantly more important as an initiator than before. It is even called by some 'pension-fund capitalism'. This means that advocates of privately funded pension provision argue for a structure of welfare/social security which would become a mechanism for expanding stock markets in order to finance production – turning the conventional understanding of the process of investment-accumulation-profit-social distribution upside-down. The method of social distribution now moves to the top of the process. In other words, as we shall see, the structure of pension provision is now supposedly a determinant of economic growth itself.

Figure 3 contrasts countries which I have grouped as Anglo-American or European. Those with large pension assets also have large stock markets. This would appear to follow from the significant

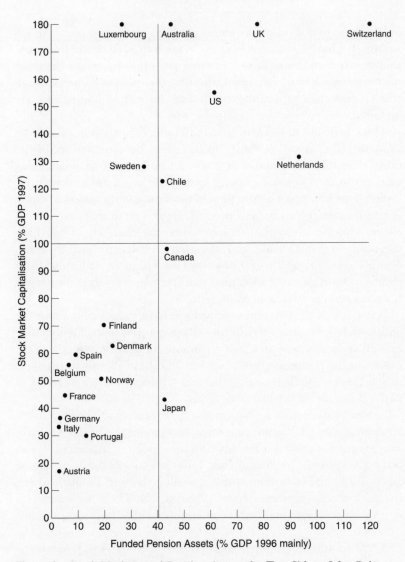

Figure 3 Stock Markets and Pension Assets: the Two Sides of the Coin

Note: stock market capitalisation = total market value of listed domestic companies.
Sources: calculations from IFC, 1998; *Economist*, 1998; and Table 2 sources.

overlap between the two. As mentioned above, for instance, the US and the UK have large stock markets in relation to GDP and their pension funds own over 30 per cent of the shares quoted on their respective stock markets; again, the figure is higher if the pension-related holdings of mutual funds and insurance companies are included.

The expansion of pension funds will indeed give a general fillip to stock markets, as prices rise from increased demand for securities, other things being equal. But it should be noted that many stock markets in developed countries were substantial relative to their underlying economies before funded pension systems added to them. It is only or mainly in the last twenty-five years or so that the pension system and the stock markets have come together. This underlines the point that historically countries have tended to have different overall economic and social philosophies within capitalism when it comes to both the role of capital markets *and* the significant social transfers represented by pension systems.

A few points of note and qualification have to be made about the figure. First, Scandinavian countries (the legendary 'social democratic' model) do seem to be in a half-way house, or at least a 'quarter-way' house. In the figure they are placed in a position slightly to the right of the European cluster in the bottom left-hand corner in terms of pension assets and stock-market values.

Second, Luxembourg's high stock-market rating relative to GDP is an anomaly. Its GDP is tiny and many companies use its stock market for registration purposes because of favourable tax treatment. It can boast 220 banks from 25 countries, 1,400 investment funds managing assets of LFr 12,500 billion, and as a result is the world's tenth largest financial centre (*Financial Times,* 1998e, p. 27). These are enormous figures for a continental European country with a population of less than 400,000.

Third, in the previous typologies of financial systems, Japan is frequently classified as one of the exemplars of the bank-based approach, but I have classified it as a member of the Anglo-American pensions bloc. Perhaps its relatively low stock-market value shown in the diagram questions my classification. Unfortunately, markets can go down as well as up, as we are reminded by the market crashes of 1997–99, and also as we read in the majority of investment prospectuses seeking money. The Japanese market fell by 28 per cent in 1997 (while the US market rose by 30 per cent). Nevertheless, the Japanese market is still the second-largest in the world. Japan has also been steadily adopting Anglo-American financial practices by introducing changes to banking and financial market activity, partly as a result of pressure from the US to 'open up' its markets, including its financial services. It is an interesting case study because of the way in which a corporate system of interlocking shareholdings has existed alongside an expanding stock market.

However, there is another point to be made about Japan, and that concerns the gradual unravelling of the interlocking shareholdings of the famous *keiretsu* groups of banks and industrial companies – one of the foundations of the bank/credit-based structure. A report by UNCTAD has suggested that recent cross-border sales of Japanese companies (mergers and acquisitions) may indicate 'fundamental changes in Japanese corporate culture, structure and strategies'. The corporate structures of the *keiretsu* have been re-evaluated, the report argued. It gave the example of Yamaichi Securities. When this went bankrupt in 1998, no related firms from the Fuyo group, of which it was a member, attempted a rescue. Instead it was bought by Merrill Lynch of the United States, one of the largest fund managers (and pension-fund managers, Merrill Lynch-Mercury) in the world. In addition, sales of cross-holding stocks owned between banks and industrial companies in Japan reached record levels in 1998. The proportion of the stocks of industrial firms owned by banks as a percentage of total stocks declined to 40 per cent, compared to 44–5 per cent in the early 1990s. Stocks of banks owned by industrial companies declined from 16.5 per cent to 15 per cent (UNCTAD, 1999, p. 97). These are not enormous changes, but they may indicate a trend. Whether or not they are 'fundamental' we shall have to wait and see.

Andrew Leyshon traces the changes in the Japanese financial system back to the early 1970s,

> since when it has been undergoing a far-reaching process of restructuring, which has served to transform its postwar growth model. In short, the Japanese financial system has become less distinctive and has come to resemble the financial systems of other core capitalist systems [in particular, the United States].
>
> (Leyshon, 1994, p. 117 [and later])

The figures can only be indicative of my contention that the nature of financial systems and pension arrangements are significantly related. If they are as I contend, this relationship has implications for corporate systems, investment, capital–labour relations and economic growth as well as pension benefits, and the relationship between financial systems and welfare/social security, as I will try to demonstrate. The Japanese example of cross-border acquisitions by US companies and others also throws up an international dimension more generally, to which I shall return.

To sum up. There appears to be a system of capitalism or economic development which makes pensions/social security centrally dependent on the nature of the finance/production system, and in turn, a determinant, or very important partial determinant of it. In a nutshell, the financial system and the pension system emerge as virtually two sides of the same coin. My thesis is, therefore, that *finance/production relationships and pensions and the financing of pensions do not exist independently of each other*. Of course, whether or not all the presumptions and claims that are made for this comprehensive structure of pensions/finance/production as exemplified by the Anglo-American model are 'true' is another matter.

So let us now consider some of the claims that are made about the Anglo-American model in more detail to discover more about the links between pension arrangements and considerations about the financing of production and economic growth.

4

The Opposing Claims of the
Welfare Blocs

Before we examine the opposing claims in a technical sense, I want to make a few initial remarks concerning the role of the financial sector which may help to provide some background to the forthcoming arguments.

BASIC ASSUMPTIONS AND CLAIMS

As is now widely known, forecasts of the increasing numbers and proportions of retired people have raised fundamental questions about the costs of financial support for pensioners. They have also raised questions about the diminishing returns on public money which are said to result from state retirement systems. Indeed, the World Bank has gone so far as to suggest that there may be state budget crises caused by the 'soaring' pension liabilities of governments and their pay-as-you-go systems.

Instead, it is proposed that financial institutions should assume substantial responsibility for pensions. Countries should provide privately run and privately invested retirement savings plans which will produce rates of return on the nation's capital which the state, for various reasons, it is alleged, cannot. This will apparently lessen the growing expense of old-age provision. In fact, a whole theory of economic development has emerged based upon the private provision of pensions through financial institutions and investment on stock markets.

Essentially, systems which are run by the state and which are also funded, or invested by the state, are criticised by supporters of the Anglo-American model because they leave little or no room for financial institutions. For example, by 1996, Singapore was the fourth-largest foreign exchange trading centre in the world, the fifth-largest trader in derivatives and the ninth-largest offshore lending centre. The Government of Singapore Investment Corporation is increasingly using private-sector managers, but its $48 billion Central Provident Fund (CPF) for pensions is managed by a state body. This situation in Singapore may be changing as the government looks at the possibility of private management of the CPF as an important attraction for further expansion of the country's financial markets.

However, the CPF has been singled out by the Adam Smith Institute in the UK for unfavourable comparison with the privately managed system in Chile. The Institute claimed that 'UK pension managers could probably run rings round the Singapore CPF' (Butler et al., 1995, p. 8). At the same time, it should be noted, a major UK pension-fund manager and historic merchant bank called Barings was being sunk in Singapore. One trader in Singapore incurred losses of over $2 billion through speculation in Japanese stock market futures, which was unauthorised trading, not checked by independent bookkeepers and financed by Barings in London without their questioning the use of the money and the steadily rising losses which were hidden away in secret accounts. What remained of Barings, after belated boardroom resignations, was acquired by the Dutch bank ING for one pound (GBP), ironically returning Barings, such as remained, to its origins in the Netherlands. Creditors of Barings declared subsequently that they planned to sue the Bank of England for inadequate supervision of the merchant bank.

Such events, however, are dismissed as exceptions which allegedly prove the rule. They are attributed to 'rogue traders' and therefore do not challenge the basic thesis. What then happens when the whole market is caught out, as in the emerging market mania and crash of 1997–98, is something which we will examine later. It is not so easily dismissed as an exceptional event, unless the whole market consists of 'rogues'! But then the logic starts to get a little difficult to sustain – unless we change a few assumptions.

Furthermore, the World Bank and others suggest that state-run investment plans, such as provident funds, can be a 'backdoor to nationalisation'(World Bank, 1994, p. 214), although they do not appear to add much explanation as to what they mean by this apparently pejorative implication. When commenting on the state managing and investing US social security (pension) funds, Martin Feldstein remarks that 'At a time when the world is moving away from state ownership, it would be a mistake for the US government to effectively nationalise almost half of American business' (Feldstein, 1997a, p. 35). Why such a move would be a 'mistake' is not explained. The assertion that 'the world' is not doing it is also not particularly persuasive. Moreover, why shares in companies held by a public trust fund amount to 'nationalisation' is left unexplained. I will come back to the implication of alleged political 'interference' later. For the time being, let it rest that the allusions, innuendoes and arguments used by some academics and the World Bank itself are extremely tendentious and disappointing.

The Chilean scheme, in contrast, with individualised savings accounts run by financial institutions, was introduced in the early 1980s. The exercise was part of a broader attempt to apply what has become known as the 'Chicago School' of economics (or what Doug Henwood calls the 'Chicago-school dictatorship' – Henwood, 1998, p. 304). The Chilean pension scheme is applauded by the World Bank (1994) and is being copied or adapted by other countries in South America (see Caufield, 1997, for the politics of the World Bank in relation to Chile; for social policy developments in Latin America, see Huber, 1996). US fund managers are reported to have captured over a third of the new pensions' business in Chile, and Chilean pension funds in turn are reportedly collecting business in Eastern Europe.

The arrangements in Chile are often seen as very positive in the sense of making the break between the old pay-as-you-go and the new funded systems. This means that the period of transition was arranged so as to avoid the expense involved in the change of pension systems. This refers to the costs involved in ending one scheme, with its liabilities for current and future pensioners, for which current contributors or taxpayers must pay, while establishing a new scheme in which current savers are separated from future obligations for others.

Very good in theory, it appears. According to Michael Littlewood (1998) (I believe he is quoting other authors in his discussion), the transition costs in Chile incurred by the move from the old to the new system are:

> after fifteen years, still *five per cent of GDP* and there is disagreement as to when that figure will decrease. The change both forced the government to run budget surpluses and to redirect spending away from other areas of need. Some commentators [UNDP is referred to in a footnote] are now saying that the transition costs will never disappear . . .
>
> (Littlewood, 1998, p. 86, my emphasis)

This is interesting, since many commentators, including the World Bank, applaud Chile for making such a fundamental financial transformation in its pension system. The figure of 5 per cent of GDP is, however, instructive for changing a pension system. By comparison, in the early 1990s, I recall that the German government was spending around 7 per cent of GDP on the considerable task of the reconstruction of former East Germany and its reunification with West Germany. Switching to a private arrangement is therefore, by implication, very costly.

Systems which are not invested or funded, but are not run by the state, are also subject to criticism, because they do not involve investment at all (apart from cash balances). The French system is run by employers and representatives of employees, is based on contributions, is earnings-related, but includes pay-as-you-go principles. The German system has relied on the book reserve system, in which companies retain future pension commitments on their balance sheet and do not hand over the contributions to capital markets.

Some funded systems which are run by the state or state institutions (ostensibly), such as the states and local government schemes in the US and the UK, remain largely free from criticism, because they delegate control of investment, for the most part, to private financial institutions. When the state does get involved, it is subject to charges of political interference, such as the policies of states in the US designed to oppose the apartheid regime in South Africa (Feldstein, 1997a), or policies of local government funds towards the promotion of the local economy and employment, especially when employees and retirees (beneficiaries) are involved in the decision-making process (Davis, 1995). In other words, there should be no 'interference' by non-financial people in either investment decision-making or in market criteria as determined by some supposedly objective criteria.

I have addressed some of these issues elsewhere (in relation to the role of employees and contributors in the UK, see Minns, 1996b). I shall also maintain later that other arguments are based on narrow definitions of rates of return as determined by stock-market criteria and are inadequate for the assessment of overall 'rates of return' and GDP growth which, in real terms, benefit pensioners and future pensioners, however qualitative this assessment may appear to some.

As for South Africa, it is a matter of opinion as to whether pension funds were far-sighted enough to disinvest from a disintegrating regime, with economic sanctions exercised against it. Arguably they helped to *lead* world opinion (including that of banks and other financial institutions) towards accepting a regime that 'the world' now recognises as the legitimate system of government. But *activity* as opposed to *passivity* appears not to be the norm or the expectation in pension-fund investment.

Other commentaries concentrate on the need for efficiency and equity, which often imply that welfare benefits, including prospective benefits from pensions, may apparently have adverse effects on work, the search for work and the acquisition of skills (Esping-Andersen, 1996, foreword by Dharam Ghai, Director, UN Research Institute for Social Development, p. viii). One might counter that if the economy inequitably puts people on to welfare then perhaps action is required on the economy, not on the welfare or pensions systems. The latter are only reflections of the economy, not its determinants. But of course this gets to the core of the argument – what determines what? It reflects the controversies which are part of the differing arguments, philosophies and ideologies of the Anglo-American and other opposing models, to which we now come.

What, then, do proponents of the Anglo-American stock-market model of capitalism claim as the empirical or theoretical basis for their approach? Many of the arguments are spelled out in various publications to which I have already referred, or which are additionally contained in the references and notes below. Many of my points are drawn from, or are responses to, the World Bank report (World Bank, 1994) and associated sources which I have also summarised and referred to in other work (Minns, 1996a and 1996b).

THE CORE ARGUMENTS

The main attacks from the Anglo-American lobby are, unsurprisingly, aimed at the structure and philosophy of pay-as-you-go pension systems, along with the role of the state in welfare/pensions provision.

The arguments are extensive and often intense. Variously, they claim the following:

1. Demographic changes, leading to ageing populations, are undermining pay-as-you-go systems and the ability of governments to maintain benefits, as the ratio of workers to pensioners declines – in relative terms, fewer people earning have to pay for more who are not.

2. The present value of state pension benefits scheduled to be paid between now and 2030 or 2150 (two of the dates often referred to) exceeds the present value of expected contributions by two or three times the value of present GDP for most OECD countries. Although this is a bit tortuous, what it really means is that taxation or contributions (payroll taxes) will have to increase significantly to pay for the promised benefits.
3. State expenditure on pensions is already too high, it is said, at 12–15 per cent of GDP in the European Union for example, making up half or more of individual governments' social expenditure. In 'transition' and 'developing' economies the levels of expenditure mean that pension systems are supposedly bankrupt and are, in turn, bankrupting their governments.
4. Anyway, the state is unreliable, does not honour its commitments, is also frequently corrupt and (not surprisingly, I suppose) is politically motivated.
5. The state is often restrictive towards the private sector while the free movement of capital is the engine of economic growth.
6. In effect, the state crowds out the ability of private individuals to save and invest more effectively for their retirement.
7. Only the – relatively – unconstrained private sector can create and use savings for increasing investment and growth through its financial markets.
8. Thereby the private sector will create the economic growth from which rising social security and pension claims can be met.
9. In the process the private sector liberates people from dependency on the state, thereby increasing choice and self-reliance.

The arguments, of course, have their subtleties and different nuances, depending on the source. But the general thrust is consistent with a particular theoretical/ideological point of view which promotes the role of the private sector and stock markets in welfare/pensions/social security provision.

A recent article by Peter Peterson (1999) predicts some dire

consequences which will result from the ageing of populations, especially in developed countries. He looks at the implications not only for
public expenditure but even for immigration, military preparations
and international relations. This underlines the intensity of the
debates about expenditure on public pensions. It is not just an academic subject. Peterson was described in his article as Chairman of the
Council on Foreign Relations as well as Deputy Chairman of the New
York Federal Reserve Bank and Chairman of a private investment
bank. He was also Chair of the journal *Foreign Affairs*, which has produced a number of articles on the pensions debate in the last few
years, and in which the article quoted here appeared. In addition, he
headed the Concord Coalition, which examined the social security
and Medicare system and recommended some redistributive measures (Myles, 1996, p. 135).

Peterson calls for a global summit meeting to address the looming crisis. He describes the 'unprecedented economic burden on
working age people' caused by the demographic crisis (ibid.,
p. 44). Official projections, he warns, show that developed countries must pay an extra 9–16 per cent of GDP simply to meet old-age
benefit promises. What was aggravating the situation was also the
'aging of the aged'. 'The "old old" consume far more health care
than the "young old" – about two to three times as much' (ibid.,
p. 44).

Because of the growing worker shortage in relation to expenditure
requirements, we in addition face growing immigration pressure, he
argued. This is where some interesting political implications of this
whole debate have started to surface.

Immigrants are typically young and tend to bring with them the family
practices of their native culture – including higher fertility rates. In many
European countries non-European foreigners already make up nearly 10
per cent of the population. This includes 10 million to 13 million
Muslims . . . Global aging and attendant labor shortages will ensure that
immigration remains a major issue in developed countries for decades to
come. Culture wars could erupt over the balkanization of language and

religion; electorates could divide along ethnic lines; and emigré leaders could sway foreign policy.

To pay for promised benefits through increased taxation is unfeasible. Doing so would raise the total tax burden by an unthinkable 25–40 per cent of every worker's taxable wages – in countries where total tax rates sometimes already exceed 40 per cent. To finance the cost of these benefits by borrowing would be just as disastrous. Governments would run unprecedented deficits that would quickly consume the savings of the developed world.

(ibid., pp. 46–7)

There are only a few exceptions to this scenario, Peterson continues. Australia, the UK and Ireland are in a much different situation – not for demographic reasons, but because they made 'timely' policy reforms, including the introduction of 'modest' pension benefit formulas and 'new personally owned savings programs that allow future public benefits to shrink as a share of average wages. This approach may yet be emulated elsewhere' (ibid., p. 47).

The European Union must wake up to the situation, he argues. It does not even include unfunded pension liabilities in the official EMU (European Monetary Union) debt and deficit criteria for membership. This 'is like measuring icebergs without looking below the water line' (ibid., p. 48). Economies could implode and governments collapse as debt mounts and deficits escalate, he suggests.

The final warning is that falling birth-rates, together with increased demand for young workers, will also inevitably mean smaller armies to face the burgeoning threats from rogue states and terrorists. With fewer soldiers, states will have to increase technology and weaponry. But where, he asks, will the budgetary resources come from if the 'senior'-weighted electorate demands more money for hi-tech medicine?

With this sort of startling analysis it is no wonder that pension arrangements have begun to be linked to almost everything else in economic and social relations.

RESPONSES TO ANGLO-AMERICAN CLAIMS

There is a growing body of literature which offers critiques of some of these assertions, many of which are contained in more detail elsewhere.[3] My purpose here is to give a general background to my argument about the role of capital markets and the interests and arguments behind the case for privatisation of pensions/social security. What, then, are some of the initial responses to the claims of those who warn of increasing burdens and political and economic crises and who wish to privatise pensions provision through an extension of private systems?

First, there is the usual problem with statistics, predictions and attitudes towards 'old age'. Population and demography studies have a considerable history and record and constitute an academic field in their own right. They have implications for economic development, economic growth, labour markets, national savings, age structures, health, fertility and mortality, functioning of markets, welfare programmes and inequality. The results are extremely complex and in many cases inconclusive. According to one view, 'The paradox of long-term demographic forecasting is that its methods combine superb technique with an almost complete lack of predictive theory' (Eberstadt, 1997). Predictions of what will happen in 150 years' time lead me to ponder what was imagined or predicted in 1850, just before the war in the Crimea, for the coming 150 years. But now, of course, proponents of demographic forecasting might argue that we are wiser and have better technology! At least Peterson, for one, acknowledges that his figures are projections, not predictions. In addition, historically demographic figures do not show that the proportion of old people in the population has risen constantly. Attitudes towards old age are anything but unilinear and unambiguous, which means that we need to consider the particular economic and political context in which old age and pensions have currently and suddenly become so important (Conrad, 1994). We also need to remind ourselves that the boundaries between 'working age' and 'old age' are constantly shifting.

Old-age dependency ratios are also different from 'general dependency' ratios which take into account the fewer under-fourteen-year-olds in the population. There are also other dependency ratios which include the working versus non-working populations more generally. As a result, the implications for public expenditure may be nowhere near what the old-age dependency ratio implies, as put forward by its advocates (Leone, 1997). There are also 'total dependency' ratios – another variation on the theme – which appear to produce yet different results (Littlewood, 1998, p. 17). Old-age ratios also take no account of the cost of increased tax incentives or public subsidies of one sort or another implied by an enhanced private system. The present system of private old-age pensions in the UK costs the Exchequer around 12 billion GBP every year. Some estimates put the figure much higher. In the US it was estimated at $50 billion a year at the beginning of the 1990s. The introduction of personal pensions in the UK produced a net government 'loss' of 6 billion GBP between 1988 and 1993 alone.[4]

Michael Littlewood examines the various arrangements for the taxation of funded pension schemes. There are different ways of taxing these schemes. For example, a scheme can be exempt from tax on contributions, or not, exempt from tax on returns from investments, or not, or subject to tax on pensions when they are paid, or not. Where tax = T, and exempt from tax = E, most schemes are EET (contributions exempt, investment returns exempt, pensions received taxed), with the exception of New Zealand which is TTE (contributions not tax-exempt, same for investment returns, but pensions exempt). He demonstrates that EET, compared to TTE, shows a considerable net tax concession in terms of what is received by the scheme, what is accumulated at the time of retirement and what the pensioner receives as an annuity (insurance policy payments in retirement). It produces a plus 80 per cent difference for the individual contributor/retiree and a net loss on the comparison between the two tax regimes of 48 per cent for the state.

What Littlewood argues, in a very interesting analysis, is that traditional EET schemes, compared to TTE, cost current and future taxpayers 'real money'. 'That advantage is conferred on savers who use the tax-favoured vehicles – everyone pays for it, including those who save *and* those who don't' (ibid., p. 59). His overall position is against tax concessions, and I must say that, although I disagree with most of his underlying arguments about the role of the state and associated matters, his arguments about taxation (and savings and investment) are a very useful and stimulating contribution to this whole debate. His discussion of rates of return, unrestricted investment policies and the Chilean pension scheme is more problematic.

Next let us consider the concept of the impending bankruptcy of some public systems. The problem is that perceptions of the 'looming crisis' appear to be 'unrelated either to current or projected levels of expenditure on old age benefits'.

> The countries of Continental Europe face the highest levels of spending, now and in the future, in part because of generous pension schemes but also because of their very high rates of early retirement and labor force withdrawal by those under 65. Nevertheless, one hears virtually the same rhetoric of 'crisis' whether one travels to high spending Italy or to low spending Australia.
>
> (Myles and Pierson, 1998, p. 7)

Further, in 'transitional' or 'developing' economies, for instance, it is difficult to isolate pension schemes and call them bankrupt, when there are broader economic changes taking place. Although every-thing may be related to everything else, the resolution of problems concerning investment, banking, production, exports, inflation, Third World debt and other variables surely precede judgements about whether the pension system should be public or private. Unless, of course, you believe, as some privatisers appear to do, especially those from the US, that how we pay for pensions apparently determines almost everything else.

Even in 'developed' countries state expenditure on pensions is said to be 'too high'. But this depends, if true, on a subjective view about societies' preferences for public expenditure on certain activities, as well as the claim that public expenditure 'crowds out' private savings and investment and has little or a negative effect on economic demand and growth. To call future pension entitlements 'liabilities' that should be taken into account on the nation's current balance sheet is an amazing translation of complex social and political considerations and policies into a financial accounting perception of a nation, its democratic processes and its social commitments. The implication that many nations should be put into receivership (or change their policies now) because of some corporate accounting convention as applied to a nation demonstrates the ascendancy of a particular conceptualisation of the nature and measurement of welfare provision. Future liabilities (at current prices) are capitalised on the notional balance sheet, but future income is not.

Related to this, 'unreliability' in the state and state pensions can be the result of democratic accountability and changes in political priorities – the 'political risk' in pension schemes as the World Bank interestingly and tellingly calls it. On the other hand, the private sector in the UK has already produced Robert Maxwell, and also the pensions mis-selling scandal of the 1980s affecting 1.5 million people and 15–20 billion GBP of pensions. This mis-selling arose from the Conservative government's introduction of 'personal pensions'. Many contributors to occupational schemes or the state supplementary scheme (SERPS) were persuaded to leave these defined-benefit arrangements for a personal defined-contribution scheme in which the future pension was dependent on the level of contributions and returns on the stock market. The 1.5 million who became worse off were enticed by most of the leading institutions in the UK life assurance industry, which 'had developed an overemphasis on securing distribution channels rather than offering customers value for money' (Gillion et al., 2000). The new system was underpinned by subsidies from the state with inadequate regulation – which perhaps reinforces the point being made by critics of the state!

The next and fundamental point relates to the argument that privatisation will increase savings and this will support productive investment and economic growth. In the first place, whether privatisation, or the funding of pensions as opposed to pay-as-you-go, leads to increased net savings is simply not proven. Some now argue that inducing below-average earners to contribute to funded schemes will increase net savings, because this group, as yet, has little or no savings. But, if they have low income and therefore low savings, the argument may be self-defeating. Also, putting the problem of evasion to one side, even if they were able to increase savings from very low incomes, this could have a knock-on effect on those with above-average earnings who do have relatively higher savings. They may reduce their overall non-pension savings, or wealth, as they respond to the general increase in the demand for, and the price of, assets. Or, as interest rates fall in this surge of new saving, their assets appreciate in value and they increase their borrowing. This is, in other words, an extremely problematic part of the theory.

However, for the sake of the argument, let us assume that there is some positive effect on net savings. The ability of the private sector to turn these savings into economic growth through equity markets is, unfortunately, highly dubious, and is not an economic relationship which can be assessed in isolation from some other fundamental factors and definitions concerning the determinants of economic growth.

Some claim that the new savings will be invested in the most successful companies, thereby lowering the cost of capital for them. But 'successful' in stock-market terms means being able to sustain dividends or capital gains. This is not the same as promoting 'investment' or growth. And why should a lower cost of capital lead to more investment if the economy is in slump and there is no demand as a result of unemployment, declining benefits, a surfeit of savings and a government committed to cutting public expenditure? I will consider the whole argument about stock markets and the productive use of 'investment' below when we examine the various definitions of rates of return.

Further, privately funded provision, by itself and without compensating measures from the state, is not 'liberating'. This is because it creates a band of dependent people who cannot take part because of low pay or interrupted employment, especially with defined-contribution arrangements, where benefits depend on a continuing ability to make contributions to a pension plan, along with the stock-market returns on those contributions. The possibilities for redistribution within a privately funded system as such are increasingly limited, especially in these defined-contribution schemes. Also, participants in defined-contribution schemes are particularly vulnerable to penalties if they have to stop work through ill health. Defined-contribution schemes only provide participants with what they have put in plus the investment returns. These problems with contributions and investment earnings mean that the pension payment can range from 20 to 65 per cent of final salary, leading one major survey to conclude that these pensions depend on 'pot luck' (*Financial Times*, 2000d, p. 20).

In addition, referring to the arguments about choice, competition and lower costs for the consumer, up to 30 per cent of personal pension contributions can be consumed in costs; in Chile the operating costs of the private competition in 1990 was 15.4 per cent of annual contributions and 2.3 per cent of total assets. In Singapore, in contrast, where there is a public monopoly, the figures were 0.53 per cent and 0.1 per cent respectively (World Bank 1994, p. 224).[5]

I believe also that retired people should be seen (both in the narrow calculus of economics and accountancy as well as the broader politics of welfare) as part of the 'active' economy, rather than a dependent cost or a passive 'burden' whose increasing longevity also adds to their 'cost' and the nation's 'liabilities'. They spend, save and invest and may not, after all, be net consumers of public money or national wealth when we take into account the broader effects of their activities. They also perform other social, voluntary, group and family activities, such as (grand)childcare, community and charity work, all of which are not captured by quantitative measures such as GDP, or which are not set off against the devil of public expenditure, but which are crucial for many social and economic activities. This is a subject which appears to be crying out for detailed work. There is some to which I come next.

THE CRUCIAL ARGUMENT: SAVINGS AND INVESTMENT

The savings argument is indeed crucial to the private investment theory. Even the Adam Smith Institute publication on 'Singapore versus Chile' concludes that, if the argument about savings and investment falls, then so does the whole case for privatisation (Butler et al., 1995, p. 28). Martin Feldstein, a leading academic in this field and a major advocate of privatisation, seems to agree when he remarks 'Without extra savings and an increase in the nation's capital stock [undefined], nothing would be gained by shifting some of the existing trust fund [federal government social security] from government bonds to private stocks or bonds' (Feldstein, 1997a, p. 33). I suppose, in passing, this also means there should be restrictions on non-domestic, or foreign, investment since that does not increase the nation's 'capital stock' either – but that is another story.

In the view of the Adam Smith Institute authors and Feldstein, I assume that, if private savings do not lead to increased private investment, then they amount to the same as the allegedly 'unproductive' state saving which arises from increased taxation. Or, as Malcolm Crawford has described it:

> If funding does not add materially to future GDP, pensions, in the aggregate, cannot really be paid for in advance. If real GDP is not increased by funding, then funded and unfunded pensions alike have to be provided out of a total of contemporary real resources which pensions funding cannot alter. In that case, effectively all pensions are pay-as-you-go, in terms of their economic consequences. The difference is that state schemes do not have to be funded (which saves on running costs) while private ones have to be funded to ensure their solvency.
>
> (Crawford, 1997, p. 39)

To question the arguments about savings even further, Christina Oling has produced a model which, in my view, questions the so-called 'Life Cycle Hypothesis' (LCH) (Oling, 2000; inferences and generalisations from her work are mine alone). According to the LCH, broadly speaking, people are assumed to be net savers for a key part of their working life when they are earning, and then consumers of those savings in retirement when they are not, in a supposedly logical progression of saving and consumption which matches the circumstances of a working life, followed by non-working or non-income generation. Oling's model relaxes certain traditional assumptions about the supposed homogeneity of people in their saving and consumption habits, as well as relaxing certain assumptions about the efficiency of markets.

The upshot is that savings can *increase* in retirement, or at least the neat logic of the LCH is, after all, not so straightforward. The World Bank has also confirmed that the LCH is not confirmed because, as it mildly puts it, dissaving by the elderly (the net transfer of their savings from working life to consumption in retirement) 'is not observed' (World Bank, 1997a, p. 115).

Empirically speaking, in the UK a government survey has revealed that nearly one-third of retired couples have savings of over 20,000 GBP. In Italy estimates show that pensioner households save 30–35 per cent of their income on average. Another report again shows that in Britain and Italy, and also Germany and Canada, savings rates *rise* after the age of sixty-five, and that over-seventy-five-year-olds save a larger proportion of their incomes than at any time in their lives.[6]

All this could turn the whole stock-market theory on its head, yet again. The policy implication for the savings advocates would be this: if you want to increase savings, you must increase public pensions – completely the opposite of what they are trying to achieve, which is to reduce public expenditure by whatever apparent means.

In any case, savings rates comprise many things – personal, corporate and government.[7] In these debates about pensions we tend to concentrate on personal savings but there is no automatic link between *these* and investment. The closest link is between corporate savings (retained earnings) and investment. Again, the policy conclusion is the opposite of that proposed by the savings advocates. It would remove tax concessions from personal savers and use the concessions to promote higher levels of corporate retained earnings. In other words, it is not the level of national savings which is the issue, it is the *nature* of the savings.

But this in turn assumes that there are profitable investment opportunities. As one commentator has concluded (in Pollin, 1997), prospective profitability drives investment, and realised profitability drives saving. Supply of (private individual) savings does not create its own demand. This is central to Keynesian analysis (and therefore, presumably, marginal to neo-liberal, supply-side economics). (For an interesting summary of the historical debate concerning the role of savings creating its own demand and the role of this in liberal and laissez-faire economics going back over one hundred years, see Fairmount, 1996, especially pp. 198–202 and 230–41.)

The Anglo-American and neo-liberal model suggests an answer to this savings dilemma and the creation of demand. There must indeed be more action on the supply side of costs. The conditions for profitability will come from lower labour costs as a result of, first, reducing social security contributions, and, second, reducing the role of the state and its taxation. Unfortunately there is no link between the level of social expenditure contributions and the level of labour costs. Nor does it matter whether they are funded out of taxation. In any event, lower labour costs mean lower purchasing power and demand. So, relatively speaking, does a higher rate of national saving. But here we meet again the ideological divide.

For example, if it were just a matter of increasing net national saving, then another policy conclusion would be to increase taxation for a given level of expenditure. But this would be completely unacceptable to the Anglo-American theorists, because they are, in principle, anti-taxation and anti-state for other theoretical and policy reasons. Singapore has the highest savings rate in the world, and the US is among the lowest of the industrialised countries in this regard.

But little is stated about this actual experience in the abstract models of increased savings and economic growth when the relative merits of public and private pension systems are discussed.

AN APOLOGIA FROM THE WORLD BANK?

In a paper produced in 1999, of which a joint author was at the time the Chief Economist of the World Bank itself, some startling comments on the World Bank model were introduced along with some interesting references to World Bank pensions experts Estelle James and Robert Holzmann, both of whom I have quoted or referred to in this book (Orszag and Stiglitz, 1999). The paper questioned the assumptions about increases in savings and investment associated with pre-funded individual accounts, the role of the public sector, rates of return on funded arrangements and pay-as-you-go, the assessment of risk in pensions and investment, intergenerational equity, analysing these and other issues in the context of 'ten myths' about social security systems. It drew on much research and internal Bank papers which had been provoked partly by the World Bank 1994 report and suggested that the report contained 'nuances' which many interpretations of the argument, not least by the World Bank's 'leading pension scholars' themselves, failed to reflect. I find it very difficult to identify these so-called nuances in the World Bank report, and in fact the paper contained additions, modifications or reversals (to put it mildly) to the basic thesis, rather than, in my view, 'nuances'. The upshot, perhaps, was that the World Bank should start again.

I appreciate that this is a very sensitive issue for the World Bank, especially given the coverage of the 1994 report during the last five to six years and the marketing of what is now described as a partial interpretation of the report. This partial interpretation of the case for individual retirement accounts in pre-funded, privately managed arrangements, may imply or use arguments that are indeed unsubstantiated in either theory or practice. My summary here contains some of the main points from a more detailed analysis of the myths and must therefore reflect my own 'nuances'.

The ten myths are divided into three sections: macroeconomic, microeconomic and political economic. The paper describes the ten myths as follows:

Macroeconomic myths

1.   *Individual accounts raise national savings.* Here the authors distinguish between pre-funding in the narrow and the broad sense. In the narrow sense pre-funding, they suggest, may create assets from which returns can be made, but this may have nothing to do with increasing national saving – or pre-funding in the broader sense.

2.   *Rates of return are higher under individual accounts.* Among other things, the authors suggest that comparisons of rates of return between state social security pensions and individual private accounts are misleading, because returns in the long run, they argue, can only be obtained at the expense of both reduced consumption and reduced returns for intervening generations. In addition, administrative costs and transition costs are often ignored in the calculations.

3.   *Declining rates of return on pay-as-you-go systems reflect fundamental problems.* In fact, declining returns do not reflect something fundamental, only the increasing maturity of pension systems. If some generations receive 'super-market' rates of return, all others must therefore receive sub-market rates of return. 'Again, the introduction of individual accounts does not change that conclusion' (ibid., p. 20).

4.   *Investment of public trust funds in equities has no macroeconomic effects.* They point out the inconsistency in the privatisation case when its proponents argue that diversification into equities through private accounts has substantial economic and social benefits, but claim at the same time that diversification of public trust funds into similar assets has none of the same alleged advantages.

Microeconomic myths

5.   *Labour market incentives are better under individual accounts.* The conference paper states that the issue is about welfare, not labour supply. Increasing the need to save later in life through the introduction of a defined-contribution pension arrangement may, for example, encourage more saving and the labour supply, but the inherent increase in risk for the individual can have a large adverse effect on welfare.

6.   *Defined-benefit plans necessarily provide more of an incentive to retire early.* This is related to the previous myth. But, they argue, encouragement of early retirement is not a necessary component of a public defined-benefit system and research demonstrates that it does not necessarily provide a justification for moving to individual private pension accounts.

7.   *Competition ensures low administrative costs under individual accounts.* The authors refer to figures which I have already cited to indicate that this is simply not proven. They quote some other research which examined the costs of individual accounts in the UK and which estimated that, on average, between 40 and 45 per cent of the value of these individual accounts were consumed by various fees and costs, explicit or implicit.

Political economy myths

8.   *Corrupt and inefficient governments provide a rationale for individual accounts.* Maybe so, but a 'rule-based' system in which public funds are invested in government bonds or in broad market indices is relatively easy to monitor and therefore less open to abuse, while 'given the wide variety of ways in which private actors can circumvent the intent of any specific rule, a government regulatory system can be quite complex. Such complexity may increase the potential for corruption' (ibid., p. 32).

9.   *Bail-out policies are worse under public defined-benefit plans.* This means governments are supposed to face greater pressure to rescue a public defined-benefit system than a private

defined-contribution one. However, the authors suggest that private arrangements can include implicit government guarantees. 'It is simply politically unrealistic to claim that governments will fail to come to the rescue in some way if financial disaster looms for a non-trivial share of the population' (ibid., p. 34). On the other hand, governments themselves can put private funds at risk. Some arrangements in transition economies have involved pension funds in buying relatively illiquid shares from privatisation funds. 'To be sure, the pension reforms are often touted as "deepening the stock market". Yet they may ultimately merely reallocate losses from one set of funds to another – and in a potentially regressive fashion' (ibid., p. 35).

10. *Investment of public trust funds is always squandered and mismanaged.* Among other considerations, the authors rerun some of the figures from the World Bank report of 1994, adjusting for risk, and show that the returns on public pension funds were in fact much less disappointing than originally argued, moving the returns toward the average market rate and, for some countries deemed to produce negative returns in the World Bank report, even above that rate. The authors also comment on the issue of economically targeted investments (ETIs), an important subject which I wish to discuss further in another chapter. The argument of the authors is that socially inspired ETIs, where the stock-market equivalent of 'rate of return' as the justification for investment is not the main criterion, are only a small proportion of pension-fund portfolios, especially those of public pension funds which have been the subject of most of the criticism for non-commercial, social investment.

Some of the arguments are extremely interesting, one even implying that a restriction on foreign investment would help to maximise the economic and social benefits of domestic investment, a subject which we touched on in an earlier chapter when discussing Martin Feldstein's arguments for the improvement in the domestic 'capital stock'. The returns from foreign investments in a narrow sense are one thing, but they ignore the knock-on effects of investment for the national economy in which the investments are made and which cannot be simply captured in the financial rate of return for the investor, whether domestic or foreign. Some of these arguments also maintain that, generally, the state is best placed to organise the inter-generational transfer of social payments. Most of this is somewhat sacrilegious in the light of the conclusions of the 1994 World Bank report on pension systems, *Averting the Old Age Crisis*, along with much of the privatisation literature on the free movement of capital and the need for restrictions on the role of the state.

Little is said, however, about the investment implications of privatisation. Some reference is made to economic growth and 'capital stock'. But I would add a myth no. 11, such as, *Enlarged capital markets, through private individual pension accounts or other private savings, will promote economic growth* – a crucial part of the World Bank case, as confirmed in the subtitle to the 1994 report. The pensions/social security system again is on the whole isolated from the nature of the finance and production system. It is again almost a hermetically sealed system of income and expenditure dealing with pensions as opposed to the overall system of pensions, finance and production.

Nevertheless the paper attempts to debunk all the ten myths listed above and asks for a reconsideration of some basic factors concerning the need for reform which the World Bank report of 1994 advocated.

AN APOLOGIA FROM THE IMF?

Let us turn next to the International Monetary Fund. An important IMF paper has brought together a number of the arguments concerned with savings and related reforms (IMF, 1997). Some of the conclusions are interesting, especially coming officially from a publication by the IMF, the other of the so-called 'Bretton Woods institutions'.

It argues:

- it is not possible to generalise across countries about the impact of the public pension system on savings;
- some reasonably strong evidence exists that the introduction of private pension plans increases private-sector savings, but the evidence derives mainly from the US [where, incidentally, the substantial increase in personal and retirement-related savings through mutual funds in the 1990s has coincided with a negative savings rate – dropping from 6 per cent in 1993 and to less than zero by 1998, accompanied by a substantial rise in personal borrowing, allegedly wiping out the supposed savings effect];
- replacing a pay-as-you-go system with a private, defined-contribution system, along the lines of the Chilean scheme, can increase aggregate savings, but this depends on how the deficit arising from the reform is financed;
- indeed, there is no compelling reason to believe that the addition of a second-tier, defined-contribution private plan to the public system should increase savings if it is financed by diverting part of the contributions from the existing system;
- a conventional public pension reform (increase in retirement age, increase in contribution rates), which affects the cash flow and reduces the actuarial imbalances of the plan, will increase aggregate savings;
- increased tax incentives for the promotion of private systems may have such a depressing effect on public saving as to outweigh any positive effect on broader coverage in the private sector.

We therefore have an interesting situation in which the case for the privatised arrangements has become increasingly confused by various subsequent reports from World Bank and IMF staff. In order to drive the point home, let us briefly consider some further research on the whole savings argument which takes us back to original claims advanced by academics, particularly from the US. In all probability, the research from the US played a major role in advancing the Anglo-American case. This case is now seriously questioned by some of the leading institutions that originally espoused the cause.

FURTHER REFUTATIONS

Gerard Hughes (2000) considers the extensive range of evidence, articles and reports on the savings issue which has been such an important part of the Anglo-American philosophy. He examined twenty-five studies which were conducted over a period of twenty years, starting with the work of Martin Feldstein (Feldstein, 1974). Feldstein concluded that public social security depressed personal savings by 30 to 50 per cent and that in the long run it would also decrease the private 'capital stock' by 38 per cent, implying a substantial reduction in GNP.

According to two authors who re-examined Feldstein's work, these conclusions turned out to be 'unwarranted', not least because of the revelation that they were based on a computer programming error. They concluded that the evidence did not support the conclusions about savings and, if anything, showed the opposite (Leimer and Lesnoy, 1982).

Hughes comments:

> Considering the results from time-series, cross-section, and personal pension studies the balance of the evidence on the effect of different methods of financing pensions on national saving rates does not show that pay-as-you-go state pensions significantly reduce saving or that funded occupational or personal pensions significantly increase it.
>
> (Hughes, 2000, p. 58)

Hughes also draws our attention to the World Bank report itself where a special 'Issue Brief' on the 'Impact of Pension Financing on Saving' concludes:

Numerous empirical investigations (most of them based on US data) have been unable to prove conclusively that saving did, indeed, drop once pay-as-you-go programs were established . . . Analyses of saving rates in other countries yield similar conflicting results. Studies of the saving impact of old age security programs in Canada, France, the Federal Republic of Germany, Japan, Sweden and the United Kingdom found no significant impact, except for a slightly positive aggregate effect in Sweden, where the pension program is heavily funded.

(World Bank, 1994, p. 307)

Lesnoy and Leimer themselves, the original critics of Feldstein's arguments and exposers of the computer programming error, concluded later not only that the life-cycle hypothesis was lacking in predictive power, but also, like Hughes, that when all the empirical evidence is examined, from time series, international comparisons and household surveys, the effect on savings caused by, in their case, the US social security/pensions system is inconclusive (Lesnoy and Leimer, 1987, pp. 74 and 98).

So, many of the main arguments – that pensions are about increases in national savings, and that public systems depress savings while private arrangements increase them – are inconclusive, to say the least, and they are evaluated as such by the Bretton Woods institutions themselves. They do not, in my view, provide a sound foundation for a whole theory of economic growth driven by the privatisation of social security provision. On balance, the evidence points to an opposite interpretation.

We therefore need to examine other grounds for the endurance and popularity of the Anglo-American theory among its advocates. These advocates include a wide cross-section of economic and social groups – financial institutions, governments, international government agencies, business corporations, reform groups and academics, labour and trade unions, and those who view pension reforms as essential for the introduction of a new 'risk culture' into economic systems with underdeveloped stock markets – this time trying again to forge the link between how we pay for pensions and how we finance production.

This latter factor is the crucial link, in my view, which underlies many of the arguments – the connection between the payment of pensions on the one hand and the control or financing of the corporate sector on the other.

5

The Capital-market Business

Having a home-grown investor base will not stop more Mannesmanns [hostile takeovers of German companies by UK investors]. The single [European] market will increasingly make a nonsense of borders anyway. But it will enable countries to participate more fully in *the takeover game*. Hence the extra interest in channelling pension payments through the markets as long-term (sic) funds.

(*Financial Times*, 2000e, p. 37, my emphasis)

What I now want to contend, once again, is that, essentially, the Anglo-American model of pensions provision is concerned with the expansion of capital markets. I fail to see other convincing explanations for the continuing arguments about the privatisation of pensions provision, unless indeed they are trying to achieve some other objective. I believe this other objective must be the expansion of the free movement of capital, in which the expansion of capital markets and the ability to buy and sell on these expanded stock markets at will, or almost, is an essential ingredient.

Public provision of such a large component of public expenditure and GDP which pensions represent, especially when there are clear alternatives which are marketed by the World Bank, becomes highly vulnerable when the imperative of free and expanded capital markets is introduced. Capital markets, financial market deregulation, unrestricted capital flows across markets or 'the free movement of capital' (with appropriate 'regulation', of course) are the *sine qua non* of this particular approach to economic development as a whole. The establishment and development of the capital market is seen to be, *a priori*, the defining moment of an economy according to this view of the economics and politics of growth. One only has to read a few of the documents and reports produced by the World Bank concerning the formula for economic development and transition, many of which are referred to in this book, to understand the importance the Bank places on capital-market expansion for 'developing', 'transitional' and 'developed' economies alike. We shall come across some more of these reports in Chapter 7.

This issue concerning the context of economic theory brings us squarely into the field of modern political economy. 'Economics' does not exist in a political and social vacuum. There are clear commercial, political and social interests behind the promotion of particular economic policies and, in this case, capital markets. Or, if they are not 'behind it', they support many of the arguments. They will benefit in many ways, which often, in this case, are not directly related to improving pensions. Although the intensity and comprehensiveness of these various interests are bound to vary, the presence of some or all of these interests can provide a formidable consensus for further expanding or establishing a capital-market-based pension *and* finance/production system. The World Bank is often in the background.

Let us examine each of these interests in turn. They comprise a veritable range of social, political and economic concerns; financial, governmental (national and international), corporate, labour, 'reform movement' and 'new risk culture' supporters. These interests cover most regions of the world, East and West, North and South.

FINANCIAL INTERESTS

Let us not beat about the proverbial bush. For the financial institutions, the extension of private provision of pensions through investment on capital markets is a business in its own right – they make money out of it, which it is, of course, their job to do. They are not theoreticians, philosophers, moralists or social workers. Any claim that they are runs counter to the whole free-market approach. Their *raison d'être* is to sell the basic product – which is not pensions *per se*. Eurodollars, petrodollars, pensions – the business is the money to be made out of managing the funds and trading the assets. This, it is argued, will in theory provide the mechanism for the profitable expansion of the economy and its ability to pay for welfare and social security. But, to be cynical, if this theory is shallow, there is still substantial money to be made from promoting the product.

The management fees alone, which are paid by pension contributors to the financial institutions in the Anglo-American system – the percentage take on the estimated $10–12,000 billion worldwide pension assets – are equivalent to at least twelve times the total public pensions bill in Greece, four times the total public pensions bill for Belgium, more than the figure for France and more or less equivalent to that of Germany.

To return to an earlier point in more detail, pension-fund management groups – the banks, insurance companies and others – are also heavily involved in the takeover and privatisation business. All of this is part of the process of market liberalisation, the free movement of capital and the expansion, extension and funding of capital markets.

In 1994, for example, eight out of the top ten 'external' pension fund managers (banks and so on to which the management of the funds is delegated) in the UK were part of financial groups which ranked among the top twenty advisers to takeovers. The other two were not part of larger banking groups with mergers and acquisitions activities. In the first ten years of privatisations in the UK, starting with the Labour government in 1977, nearly $40 billion was raised by the UK government at a cost of over $700 million in fees paid.

From 1977 to 1994 about $140 billion was raised from the privatisation programme, with commensurate fees for the advisers. Eight banking groups advised on the first wave of privatisations up to 1994, and four of these were among the ten external pension-fund managers in that year. Seven of the eight were among the top twenty-five. In turn, pension funds, or rather their managers, have played a major role in the investment decisions concerning takeovers and privatisations. There are clear conflicts of interest but there remains a common commercial and economic reform philosophy which rests on the expansion and operation of capital markets.

But this was only the start. From 1993 to 1998, UK governments raised another $35 billion from privatisations, while elsewhere in the European Union as a whole the figure approached $320 billion. This again demonstrates, I would suggest, the incursion of what I perceive as the Anglo-American philosophy into European economic governance. Italy and France dominated the list of privatisations in this period, with around 40 per cent of the total in value. But as in France apparently, 'Italy's bloated state sector has barely been dented' (*Observer*, 1999, p. 6 – another unbiased media description, I presume). These sell-offs provided more investments for pension funds and more fees for advisers to the governments and pension funds.

As we have already noted, we should also not ignore the substantial public subsidy which ironically, in Anglo-American anti-state-subsidy parlance, 'props up' the pension fund 'industry' and its ability to buy privatised stocks and also benefit from the government subsidies, or fees, paid to the financial advisers to the sell-off programmes. In the much-vaunted example of Chile, used as a model by the World Bank and others, 'huge public subsidies' are necessitated, leading to a '*de facto* subsidisation of private welfare' (Esping-Andersen, 1996, p. 22; for further discussion of this and the Chilean case, see Evelyne Huber's chapter in the same volume, especially pp. 164–9). All this is of enormous benefit to the existence and profits of the financial sector.

Although I accept that some of the above statements and comparisons with the circumstances of different European countries' pension systems are subjective or based on incomparable assumptions, these are nevertheless all countries with allegedly 'creaking' or 'bankrupt' pension systems in need of 'reform' because of their costs.[8] I am only questioning what constitutes the alleged 'costs' which would be saved by changing to a private system in relation to the prospective 'benefits' which will accrue to the financial sector. Of course, the fees earned from private management also add to the 'GDP' of the Anglo-American bloc itself, especially the US, where the leading financial institutions also happen to be based – a spatial or geographical factor I wish to consider in Chapter 8.

As a result of the commercialisation of welfare or social security, pension reformers and private providers are entrenched in devising more savings 'products' which distance themselves from references to the state and its various mechanisms and policies. The Chief Executive of the UK Prudential Assurance Company, the largest private insurance provider in the UK, has stated that winning acceptance of the need to save more for retirement is partly a marketing issue. 'It would be easier if people felt this was not a tax.' This 'would make it much easier to sell' (*New Statesman*, 1996, pp. 30–1).

The financial sector has self-evidently a clear interest in promoting private financial capital investment and savings 'products' rather than the almost direct equivalents of public saving and investment through taxation and public asset investment. The financial sector would not be 'commercial' if it did not propose these private equivalents of the state, which, arguably and as I have maintained, have less effect on economic performance, employment and welfare.

I suggest that the strategic objective of the financial sector, accompanied by the World Bank and the IMF, is indeed to extend capital markets wherever possible and to maximise the free movement of capital within and between those markets and the countries in which they are located. Capital-market development is an essential part of the so-called reform process. The financial sector itself may invoke theories of greater universal welfare and global happiness, but it also seeks to maximise management and trading fees and profits. Private pensions are another means of doing this. They are not an end in themselves.

They also raise the recurring issue of the relationship between finance, production and welfare. To take one recent example, pensions have become a particular issue in Germany. In 1999 there was controversy about the freezing of benefits by the Social Democrat government and the implications this had for social distribution more generally. The debate about the role of welfare expenditure and the nature of the financing of production had seriously taken off.

Three years previously, an economist from Deutsche Bank put the issue succinctly in an article in the *Financial Times*. The article was entitled 'A Boost for Capital Markets'. The article claimed:

> If private pension provision took off in Germany, the country's capital markets would benefit significantly. German companies have huge internal pension reserves ...
>
> By setting aside these 'book reserves' for retirement commitments, companies defer tax liabilities and have a ready-made source of finance ... 'If this money was put into the capital market, it would be used much more efficiently' [the economist from the Bank said]. Instead, the reserves ... are generally used to finance companies' own investments.
>
> The absence of these funds from the market ... 'is a significant structural hindrance to the development of German financial markets', adds Mr Schrader [economist at Deutsche Bank Research].
>
> (*Financial Times*, 1996b, p. 19)

To be cynical, one might question how devastating for the German economy this might be, to have the stock market rather than companies themselves responsible for 'corporate investment'. The argument again implies that without substantial capital markets there is a detrimental effect on economic efficiency. This is an interesting summary of the conflict between the different approaches to finance and production, of the financial side in the welfare/finance/production nexus.

The *Financial Times* also emphasised later that the state system in Germany was, as usual, 'creaking badly' (*Financial Times*, 1999b). Reductions of benefits had 'hardly mitigated the burden on German finances'. Deutsche Bank is quoted again as advising that the introduction of pension funds 'holds opportunities for the German capital market . . . A strong capital market, capable of providing the industries of the future quickly and efficiently with capital, is a key to prosperity and higher employment.'

The Bank noted that (by the end of the 1990s) 'pension fund assets in Germany are equivalent to 5.5 per cent of Germany's gross domestic product against nearly 90 per cent in the UK and the Netherlands'. The *Financial Times* concluded:

> Until pension funds enjoy the same tax status as other types of old-age financing, high hopes are being pinned on the AS funds [*Altersvorsorge-Sondervermögen* – old-age provision funds introduced by some companies] . . . They are angled towards assets such as equities and property to encourage Germans away from their safety-first preference for fixed interest savings.
>
> One big company which has decided to offer employees the opportunity to invest in AS funds is Daimler-Chrysler. DIT, the fund management arm of Dresdner Bank, is making its AS funds available for the purpose . . . But firm action by politicians remains essential. Without it, Germany's pension system will remain vulnerable and inefficient – disappointing today's young workers when they come to draw their retirement money.
>
> (*Financial Times*, 1999b, p. x)

Mergers and acquisitions also figure in this analysis of the German financial system. In the first half of 1999, the top five advisers in Germany were involved in fifty-eight deals valued at 130 billion Deutschmarks (DM). Deutsche Bank was top but the other four were US banks including the large US/UK pension-fund manager Merrill Lynch-Mercury, all with nearly 100 billion DM of the total for the top five (*Financial Times*, 1999b, p. ii). The growing competition between German and US and UK banks for merger and acquisition business can also be seen as part of the competition between the Anglo-American and European corporate/financial models, with increasing pressure being exerted on German banks to adopt Anglo-American-style approaches to profit-taking. The most outstanding example of this acquisition activity we shall consider in a following section, when we outline the largest takeover battle to date for a German company by a UK one, along with the role of pension funds.

One might finally therefore ask the following. The financial sector may have its own preferences for the structure of the relationship between finance and industry. It may have its own definition of financial 'efficiency' and productive capital allocation – whatever the historical evidence of GDP growth and capital investment. But why, in the process of making policy choices about capital markets and pensions, should this pensions/capital-market business be so seductive to governments and the corporate sector – and to labour?

The expansion of the financial markets is attractive to them for a variety of reasons. Often, again, the reasons have little or nothing to do with arguments for improving pensions themselves. So let us next consider the role of the state.

GOVERNMENT INTERESTS

First, the introduction or expansion of the private investment model of pensions using capital markets justifies, or provides some reasons for, freezing or cutting public expenditure, as we shall see. The expansion of the private, funded model thereby appears prudent and conservative for governments in the 1990s post-Cold War era of public expenditure restraint and individual responsibility for welfare or social security. Also this is the era of 'new' social democracy, where state spending causes unemployment and where social justice does not equate with public expenditure. There must be greater confidence in markets. In return the 'confidence' of the same financial markets is judged to be increasingly dependent on such policies when governments or central banks need to raise money or try to influence their interest rate or exchange rates.

Next, the private, funded pension arrangements are said to increase the demand for, and supply of, financial securities, thereby helping in the development of 'liquid' capital markets and the 'deepening' of financial markets. This means, I suppose, the extension of financial services and infrastructure, although the World Bank (1997a) defines it as the increased provision of bank finance for the private sector along with increases in stock-market turnover, no less. Governments and political parties see this extension or 'deepening' of the financial sector as a way of competing with other financial centres for the associated international banking, insurance and securities business – and the fees. This will help them obtain substantial revenue from the expanding international financial services, which are part of the 'globalisation' theory, for their own GDP and balance of payments. It can also be presented as increasing employment (through the expansion of the financial sector) in a post-Keynesian era of minimising demand management, public expenditure and public investment in what used to be known as manufacturing industry. Related to this, the increased savings which are supposed to flow from funding pensions should lower consumption (assuming that you use the 'net increase in savings' variant of the economic theory), thereby also reducing the balance of payments deficit and its funding by foreign debt, foreign investment or flight capital. This has been an important argument in Australia and Denmark.

Governments and commentators also see the increase in pension funds as a way of funding the privatisation of state-owned industry. The encouragement of private savings and demand for equities provides a supply of private capital which a government can exchange for shares in previously state-owned companies. By encouraging the population to pay for the assets a second time (the first through taxation, the second through mandatory savings schemes – or taxation by another name), governments can respond further to the general pressure to reduce the public side of the national balance sheet.

The Chairman of the Warsaw Stock Exchange has stated, albeit anecdotally, that securing enough buyers for privatised assets is exactly the reason that pension funds are needed (Butler, 1998, p. 56). Since Poland has been a major recipient of Western reform proposals and money, and is high on the list of former Communist countries for accession to the European Union, the public statement from such an important person in the general reform process in the region must be taken seriously. Indeed, supporting the privatisation process may be an argument for pension reform in Central and Eastern Europe more generally – a point to which we now come.

INTERNATIONAL GOVERNMENT ORGANISATIONS

By this title I mean the following organisations: the World Bank, the IMF, the ILO, the OECD and the EU, and their involvement in the process of 'policy transfer'. This process involves financial and technical assistance, and structural adjustment programmes of a voluntary or 'coercive' nature (see Dolowitz and Marsh, 1996, for further discussion).

First, how in practical terms does the process operate?

I like the idea of 'social movements for global capitalism', as explained by Leslie Sklair (1997). This article describes the interesting concept of an international capitalist class, comprising executives from trans-national companies, public employees, politicians and professionals and the private sector. From an organisational point of view, they provide the personnel for the process of policy transfer. They are a growing and important group of people with common business degree qualifications, world-views and consumption requirements and interchangeable employment positions.

This process of transferring policies from one country to another in the post-Communist era of 'transition' works as if comparative local circumstances were the same or similar: Albania, Bulgaria, Russia – they all are the same because they were all Communist. Therefore, the solution to their problems must be the same or very similar, and the people sent in to implement the process to a large extent share the same approach to the ideology of the reform process. Furthermore the process 'is underpinned by pluralist assumptions and the key question of whose interest is served by this process goes unasked' (Dolowitz and Marsh, 1996, p. 343). In this context of international policy transfer, these authors refer to 'too much positivism': 'few scholars look at how the definitions of problems or solutions are socially constructed' (ibid., p. 357). In other words, there are no objective solutions. There are only answers based on constellations of interests, particularly as represented now by the competing roles of the international government organisations.

A very important contribution to this issue is as follows. Robert Holzmann from the World Bank writes that, from the beginning of 'market orientation'(an interesting concept), the countries of Central and Eastern Europe were 'made aware by the IMF and the World Bank of the unsustainability of the inherited pension scheme' (Holzmann, 1997a, p. 203). In contrast, the ILO, the OECD and the European Commission recommended a more cautious approach and much less drastic reductions in (public) expenditure.

The countries of Central and Eastern Europe, Holzmann continues, were initially attracted to a European model because of their proximity to EU countries, along with the long-term presence of the ILO (which was one of the few international institutions which had a long connection with them when they were under Communism) and a desire for accession to the EU themselves. The EU countries also promised technical and financial assistance if their pension schemes were used as a model. However, many compromises ensued, partly for political reasons. The transfer of an EU variant of pension policy was, basically, not successful. Moves towards private funded systems were introduced, to a greater or lesser extent.

Holzmann explains:

> any traditional reform necessarily means a cutback of 'acquired rights' for important segments of the population, [but] neither a consensus nor a majority solution could be achieved.
>
> This may be a major reason why proposals and plans for a more drastic reform approach, moving towards a funded scheme, took hold. *Moving to*

private and funded, contribution-related schemes may prove more credible since the future benefit is considered to be dependent on the individual contribution effort and not on political distribution considerations.

(Holzmann, 1997a, p. 205; my emphasis)

Moreover,

Such thinking was certainly fostered by the World Bank Report of 1994, the positive assessment of the Chilean experience . . . and the positive externalities expected from such a reform approach on saving and capital formation, financial market developments, and labour market performance.

(ibid.)

In other words, the World Bank, and not just the ILO, was now present in these countries to market its philosophy. When push comes to shove, one must ask which of the two organisations has more influence in real political and economic terms.

Furthermore, the argument continues, the financing of the deficit incurred by the transition to a funded system ('operational deficit and compensation for acquired rights' of contributors to existing pension plans) could be dealt with by following the logic of the general economic reform and transition process ('liberalisation, privatisation and institution building', ibid., p. 205): 'all countries share the optimism that assets put forward for privatisation could help to finance the transition deficit' (ibid., p. 207).

So here we have the squaring of the political circle as implied by the World Bank (although Holzmann's article contains the disclaimer that he is writing on his own account). Private, funded pension plans are needed, it appears, in order to cut public expenditure on state systems. Privatisation of state assets is also needed in order to cut public expenditure and raise money. Private pension funds are then needed (as in the statement by the Chairman of the Warsaw Stock Exchange) in order to buy these privatised assets. The cycle of 'reform' is complete and I suppose, in this context, self-financing.

If one substitutes for 'mandatory, private, funded plans' the expression 'taxation by another name', then the overall structure of payments is just the same. But the political conundrum of first, raising money and cutting public expenditure, or of cutting 'taxation' and benefits, and then second, of privatising assets and benefit claims, has been solved. It has been solved by the promotion of the private domestic financial sector and the marketing, by the World Bank and others, of the unproven theory of pension funds and their alleged beneficial effects for economic development (savings and 'capital formation').

This may amount to nothing less than a façade for a deeper process of change in which the politics of 'reform' and expansion of capital markets, as required by the World Bank and the IMF, demand a fundamental change in the balance between the public and private sectors (Figure 4), whatever the consequences for the real economy. The issue becomes political, not economic.

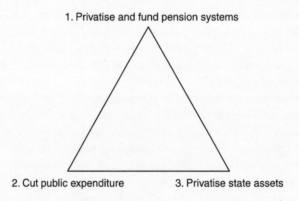

1. Privatise and fund pension systems

2. Cut public expenditure   3. Privatise state assets

Figure 4   The Privatisation Triangle

CORPORATE INTERESTS

Moving down to the micro-level, individual companies themselves regard the expansion of domestic capital markets as a way of securing access to cheaper capital for corporate investment. This perception has increased sharply in Western Europe itself following German unification and the expansion of the EU, along with corporate expansion into Central and Eastern Europe, post-1989.

Ironically, some companies view the expansion of their domestic financial institutions as a way of countering the international expansion of *other* countries' pension funds – mainly, but not solely, US pension funds which are buying the shares of European companies and seeking to change the voting rules to give more power and rights to shareholders. The leader in the field in this regard is CalPERS – the pension fund of the state of California, which has a clear and publicly declared strategy of identifying companies in the US and abroad which appear to 'underperform' relative to the assets underlying their share price. The assets, and therefore the company as measured by share value, are deemed to be undervalued according to their underlying and saleable asset value.

This is certainly an 'active' investment strategy but I am uncertain as to what the 'underlying' economic, as opposed to shareholder, benefits are supposed to be. I am not trying to be negative, I only want to question whether the primacy of shareholder rights, or 'unlocking shareholder value', is the same as, or leads to, the prioritisation of general economic and social development. My feeling is that it does not. But perhaps we have to wait for the evidence.

In 1998, CalPERS joined forces with Hermes – the UK British Telecom (BT) pension-fund management institution – in a combined so-called Anglo-American 'corporate governance' strategy. These funds are among the largest pension funds in the US and the UK (some figures show them to be the largest in their respective countries). Together, the two funds control assets of $198 billion, and each fund holds around 1 per cent of their respective domestic equity markets, which represents enormous market power. This seems like the epitome, in an institutional sense, of the consolidation of the Anglo-American approach to corporate philosophy, involving the use of pension funds in the relationship between finance and production.

Another joint venture established in 1998 was Hermes Lens Asset Management. By the end of 1999 this had accumulated ten pension-fund investors from the US, UK, Canada and, interestingly in the light of our earlier discussions about the classification of different models, Scandinavian countries. The aim of the company was to extend its investment activity in 'underperforming equities' into continental Europe. The investors included the BT pension fund, five UK local authority pension funds, CalPERS from the US, Ontario Municipal Employees Fund from Canada, and SPP, the largest life and pensions insurance company in the Nordic region.

Without taking sides, I would suggest that their strategies are opposed to, for example, continental European corporate values. These values do not give such primacy to the stock-market valuation of corporate worth, as we have discussed earlier in our comparison of the different models of finance/production relationships. For the foreign pension funds, this activity of buying the shares and pressing for greater shareholder rights in order to change management or the use of assets increases the value of their shareholding. It makes the shares, and the company, more marketable in stock-exchange terms.

This activity represents the institutionalisation of conflict over the corporate surplus between shareholders and company management. For the companies concerned this is a threat to be countered by trying to generate domestic shareholders through the local funding of pensions provision. In France this has been a particular issue in the latter part of the 1990s, especially over proposed purchases or actual incursions into the purchase of significant stakes in French companies by the Americans and others. By 1999 foreign investors held over 30 per cent of French quoted company shares. The *Wall Street Journal Europe* has reported on the rising profile of buyout funds – those packs of private capital that prey on juicy assets that are prime for a quick makeover and a resale to the highest bidder. The fast-moving funds typically boast returns of 30% a year . . . What's driving all this? US pension funds and other big investors, encouraged by talk of widespread restructuring within Europe's sclerotic conglomerates, have been investing in private equity as never before . . . Propelling the flow of cash is an appetizing blend of low interest rates, stable inflation and the maturing European capital markets.

(*Wall Street Journal Europe*, 1999, p. 1)

It added that fund-raising for private equity was less than $5 billion a year for the period up to 1997, but for 1998 and 1999 it was running at up to $20 billion per year. France and Germany were apparently favourite target countries. The important players also included British pension funds and US/UK pension fund managers such as Merrill Lynch-Mercury.

The first example of the power of pension funds in the year 2000 was revealed by the attempted hostile takeover by the UK company Vodafone AirTouch of the German company Mannesmann, in the telecommunications/engineering/steel sectors. This hostile takeover also revealed another incursion of the Anglo-American model of shareholder markets in corporate control, of buying and selling companies, into the continental European model, relatively unfamiliar with such means of corporate change or transformation. Again the link between the corporate/finance relationship and the role of pension funds with their associated social security system is revealed, in this case, as we have seen before, in the creeping transfer of Anglo-American standards to the European model of financial and industrial relationships.

The Vodafone takeover was the largest takeover ever recorded and it was the first time a foreign company had successfully launched a hostile bid for a large German company. The sum paid was equivalent to nearly three times the GDP of Chile and over 10 per cent of the GDP of the UK. The fees generated for the banks and other advisers to the deal were estimated to amount to nearly 600 million GBP. The *Financial Times* remarked:

> It is a deal that will throw open the corporate doors of Europe and pave the way for a wave of cross-border mergers and acquisitions . . . It demonstrates that there are no longer any no-go areas as European business embarks on a widescale restructuring . . . One investment banking adviser to Vodafone said: 'Germany's hitherto unbreachable corporate world has finally been broken and many are going to be licking their lips.'
>
> (*Financial Times*, 2000a, p. 1)

More to the point, for our analysis:

> the lack of a proper funded pensions system in Germany creates an ownership vacuum. While domestic shareholdings in large listed companies are often highly concentrated, it is not uncommon for more fragmented foreign shareholdings to account for 40 or 50 per cent of the outstanding equity. This leaves companies vulnerable to takeover once the principle of an active market in corporate control is accepted . . . And attempts to overhaul a welfare system that imposes heavy costs on companies have produced modest results.
>
> (ibid., p. 18)

Following the takeover, the German Chancellor set up a special committee to examine whether any action should be taken to restrict such bids. The British Prime Minister, on the other hand, argued that the takeover was a part of the growing European single market. He suggested that shareholder power should be respected by governments. Next in line, the Mannesmann employee representatives on the company's supervisory board warned Vodafone about the possibility of conflict with the workforce.

Back in the US, TIAA-CREF, arguably the world's largest pension fund, supported the Vodafone takeover, pledging its 1 per cent of Mannesmann shares for the deal. In contrast, the US AFL/CIO congress of trade unions – presumably in touch with the German trade unions – warned about the commercial dangers of the potential deal and urged the managers of its benefit funds to oppose the takeover. AFL/CIO's investment department provided corporate governance advice to a number of collectively bargained benefit funds, and these in turn owned or controlled around 13 per cent of Mannesmann shares. This was an important position to hold, especially since the non-German shareholders in Mannesmann had begun to outnumber the Germans. Pension funds and other UK and US investors with a European investment strategy were bound to have some stake in Mannesmann, given its importance in the large telecommunications and European engineering market. During the takeover controversy Mannesmann had also acquired Orange, a successful mobile tele-phone company, incidentally further increasing the number of non-German shareholders in Mannesmann itself. Vodafone eventually 'won'.

All this is not to say that domestic pension funds are always seen as the answer in defensive strategies. But the perception of significant threats to a corporate culture allegedly very different from Anglo-American shareholder value priorities, lies behind a number of corporate statements about the need to protect the continental European corporate economy from the hostile takeovers coming from US and UK companies and pension funds.

The defensive strategy of establishing domestic pension funds implies one or more of at least four assumptions: 1. It assumes that domestic shareholders will be more sympathetic to domestic man-agers. I am not sure, however, whether the assumption of patriotism or national sentiment in the operations of finance and pension funds is sustainable. 2. It assumes that the share prices will rise as more investors enter the market, thereby undermining the objective of the pension-fund raiders. But perhaps this may create a subsequent capi-tal loss for domestic funds if prices then fall. 3. It assumes solidarity between pension funds – we will not sell our shares in your company if you do not sell your shares in ours – a scenario which conjures up a 'prisoners' dilemma' for domestic funds. 4. It assumes that employers will invest the bulk of 'their' particular pension fund in the shares of their own company as a blocking tactic – an extremely controversial proposition politically and one which would also take some time to accomplish in practice.

Let us consider the extent of the Anglo-American bloc 'threat' to the European bloc. Seven out of the ten top multinational companies, ranked by foreign assets, are from the Anglo-American bloc – namely from the US, the UK, the Netherlands and Switzerland. They employ more than a million people outside their 'home' country. No less than 90 per cent of the top 100 multinationals with foreign assets are from so-called 'Triad' countries – the US, European countries and Japan (UNCTAD, 1999, p. 78). In Europe, foreign direct investment funds from the UK amounted to 30 per cent of the European total.

All this means that the influence of pension funds internationally is not just confined to flows of pension-fund capital from one country to another, or overseas portfolio investment, but is also bound up with the flows of foreign investment contained in mergers and acquisitions. This suggests another dimension to the global reach of pension-fund capitalism, particularly the spread of the Anglo-American corporate model ('the other side of the coin'), following an acquisition of a French or German company by a US or UK one, which has never seriously been taken into account. It adds an interesting feature to the analysis and growth of the pensions/corporate dualism.

If a US company buys a French company, for instance, the French company may no longer have a share quotation on the French Bourse, but the US company *does have* a quotation – on the New York Exchange, where pension-fund shareholders will play an important role in share pricing and possible activist strategies before and after the acquisition.

This is indeed the essential purpose of the defensive strategies discussed above – to develop the capital market by promoting domestic pension funds in order to avoid being taken over by the complex of the stock markets/pension funds/corporate model of other countries. This is self-defeating, of course, because of the pressure the domestic markets, with their new pension-fund portfolio approach, will in turn put on domestic corporate relationships. But it suggests that if defensive strategies fail, we may have to qualify the dualism – corporate structures may change, but not through the rise of domestic markets and pension funds, but through those of foreigners. 'Domestic dualism' may be overtaken by an 'international dualism' in the next stage of the development of the Anglo-American model.

However, in practice the process is much more complex than this implies. For example, of the twenty largest cross-border merger and acquisition deals announced in 1998 and 1999 (until June 1999), only one was from an Anglo-American bloc country to a European bloc member (in fact from the UK to Sweden) (UNCTAD, 1999, p. 96). This of course pre-dates the enormous Vodafone takeover of Mannesmann. Over the longer term, deals have flown both ways across the Atlantic, between the US and the European bloc, between the UK and the US, and between European bloc members themselves.

The top fifty multinationals ranked by foreign assets include thirteen from the United States and five from the United Kingdom, but also thirteen 'sclerotic conglomerates' from Germany and France (eight and five respectively). In 1998–99 the 'sclerotic' group far outdid the Anglo-Americans in the top twenty cross-border deals. Perhaps it was because of pressure, perceived or real, from their new, activist US and UK pension-fund shareholders, who are keen on discovering undervalued assets relative to share price. But this particular explanation seems tortuous.

The presence of the European multinationals in the league tables makes the rise of 'international dualism', and the role of pension funds, complicated. It is still important on a case-by-case basis, given the dominance of the US, the UK and Japan in the overall flows, and the dominance of companies from the Anglo-American bloc as a whole in terms of the largest multinationals with foreign assets. In addition, these are the companies which already have large blocks of shareholdings held by Anglo-American pension funds. What is equally important is the perceived *threat* of the pension-fund invasion.

A fascinating instance of this perception is quoted by Robin Blackburn from the views of the president of Crédit Lyonnais of

France. Putting scepticism about motives to one side for a moment, I extract a few telling remarks and exhortations from the president's statement which reveal some interesting sentiments from someone inside the European model.

> The systematic search for the highest value possible for the shareholder is nothing other than the disguised expression of *rentier* interests, with a strong preference for the future over the present, a translation of the power of Anglo-Saxon pensioners (who are the only ones to save so strongly) over the whole of world society, in short, of old or ageing Americans and Britons to the detriment of young people of all other countries . . . Let us forget for a moment frontiers and nationalities: within each of us, to put it another way, old age is in charge of what we do . . . Indeed we find that today's workers have no say over how their savings are invested and the activities of the most powerful financial interests are legitimated.
>
> (Blackburn, 1999, p. 13)

LABOUR INTERESTS

Organised labour would obviously have some sympathy with this drum-roll for workers' rights, especially coming from a banker, whatever the motives. But labour's position is somewhat contradictory.

Sometimes there is a considered judgement that arguing for a pre-dominantly public system is simply unachievable (Australia and the UK). This is linked to the opportunity provided for unions in collective bargaining in which they can treat pensions as 'deferred' wages in times of income restraint. This, in turn, provides a major opportunity to retain and recruit members in times of falling union membership. Trade unions can supply benefits to members which the private sector has singularly failed to do, except for the well-paid minority. This enables trade unions to argue for their members 'deferring' current wage-increases in exchange for a share in capital ownership in order to provide for members' retirement incomes.

The policy suited the 1950–60s' 'Keynesian consensus' of governments and trade unions seeking to limit wage-increases today in exchange for pension benefits tomorrow. This trade-off concerning the timing of wage income was a crucial element in the development of pension funds and the idea of 'deferred wages' (Minns, 1996a).

Sometimes there is a shared concern by trade unions themselves about whether or not they should trust the state with workers' pension contributions. However, whatever the history and politics of the trade union movements, once private pension funds are established there is also then a practical and political inertia when it comes to undoing the situation. This relative inertia is explained more thoroughly by Myles and Pierson (1998) using 'path dependency' theory – the ability to reform is limited by the interests, institutions and processes which have already been established.

Nevertheless, events in Germany are once again of great interest in the comparison of financial and welfare models and the process of change. In March 2000, the historically powerful IG Metall trade union agreed a wage deal which was viewed as an uncharacteristic compromise. 'IG Metall chose compromise rather than conflict and showed a readiness to shed some of its old-style rituals,' a senior economist from Merrill Lynch was quoted as stating: 'They are finally facing reality' (*International Herald Tribune*, 2000, p. 1). The article commented:

> The tentative pact coincides with an erosion of union power and membership, as well as a sea change in this tradition-bound society. In the past year alone, more Germans for the first time invested in the stock market than belonged to unions and more now work in information technology than in the fabled auto industry . . . German unions have lost nearly 4 million members from a peak of 11.8 million just after unification. IG Metall has led the trend, losing about a third of its members in that time. A third of its current members are thought to be retired or unemployed.
>
> (ibid., and p. 14)

As part of the IG Metall deal, employers agreed to extend an early retirement programme, the so-called 'pensions at sixty' provisions which will increase employers' payments to pension arrangements. This may lead to an extension of private arrangements using stock-market investments. Whether this approach and subsequent events are consistent with the predictions of the path dependency theory, or whether they do indeed represent a 'sea change', I am not sure. I want to return to this later, because I suspect that path dependency theory takes particular policy issues as defined by their immediate interest groups rather than by broader political and economic changes which occur from time to time, and which have nothing to do with the particular policy issue at stake.

In conclusion to this section, trade unions, and left-wing governments too, may have railed against the vicissitudes of stock markets and the consequences for their members or constituents, against the ability of the markets to promote the buying and selling of companies and then to restructure them through asset and employee 'disposals'. But none appears to make the link explicitly between private pension provision or private shareholding on the one hand and the growth and activity of the markets on the other.

An interesting exception to this appeared in a debate about pensions and collectivism between Robin Blackburn and Henri Jacot, the latter being the author of the annual economic reports of the CGT (Confédération Générale du Travail) trade union in France. Jacot argued that the answer to British and American pension funds supplanting French banking complexes on the Paris Bourse was not to create French pension-fund equivalents. The result would be to replicate the speculative activity (Jacot, 2000). But this perception of the links between the various issues is rare.

To return to an earlier point, production, employment and stock-market investment are seen to be one thing, pensions and social security, another.

THE ANGLO-AMERICAN 'REFORM MOVEMENT'

As has always been the case in the development of social welfare systems, the various interest groups are supported by 'reform' movements of academics and writers. The Anglo-American model has its own body of academic and other reformers.

The particular concern of Anglo-American reformers is the balance of pension funding. Between 25 and 45 per cent of the working populations in the Anglo-American core, namely the US and the UK, are not covered by the privately operated, funded pension plans. Furthermore, the average income of pensioners in the UK comprises 40 per cent from state pensions and only 26 per cent from other pensions. In the US the figures are 42 and 19 per cent respectively. The World Bank itself opines that most OECD countries have 'weak multi-pillar systems' – meaning, I believe, that the state 'pillar' dominates in terms of income received by pensioners.

Looking at members of the Anglo-American model, only Switzerland – the inventor of the multi-pillar concept – has more than half its non-wage retirement income resulting from private pensions, probably because it has such a high average wage, relatively speaking. More people can contribute enough through private schemes to give them an adequate private pension. Elsewhere, income levels exclude significant groups from contributing enough of their lifetime earnings to qualify for an adequate private pension.

Influential social reformers rule out improvements in the basic pension or social security as unrealistic, given the current parameters of pension politics and interest groups – the US Congress and the UK government would never entertain any proposal which increased the basic pension because of the implications for public expenditure, taxation and budget deficits, it is argued.

The result is that the task of reformers has become, it appears, not to improve pensions *per se*. To put it cynically, their task in practice has become one of improving the business opportunity for financial firms and their capital markets, while juggling with the panacea of 'regulation'

of the private sector by the state. I realise that this is a provocative statement, but the net result of their proposals is to attempt to do just that,
whatever their rhetoric of '*social* reform'. There is, in other words, a prevailing methodology of reform which works within certain political
parameters that appear to go unchallenged.

THE US

In the US, the social security system (the OASDI, or Old-Age,
Survivors, and Disability Insurance) was considered by the administration to be in need of reform in the early 1990s, after suffering
previous 'crises' in the late 1970s and early 1980s. Reforms had been
instituted at that time to deal with the crises, but by the 1990s the
process started all over again.

The OASDI accounts for around one-fifth of the Federal budget
and it was forecast in the 1990s that over the next twenty to thirty
years the current surplus in the funds would be exhausted, so that so-
called payroll taxes would not meet expected obligations. The OASDI
would be in further 'crisis'; the 'burden' needed to be reallocated, in
order to avoid impending 'insolvency' (the language used in Mitchell,
Myers and Young, 1999, for example, one of the most recent books
examining a wide range of technical points in US social security
reform). The US administration appointed an Advisory Council on
Social Security (1994–96) and the Council delivered its final report in
1997.

Three proposals were submitted (explained more fully, for
example, in Mitchell, Myers and Young, 1999). The first was called the
Maintenance of Benefits plan (MB). In this, the retirement age would
be increased, taxation of benefits increased, some income from
Medicare transferred to OASDI, payroll taxes increased slightly, and,
most importantly, the investment of 10 per cent of the OASDI trust
fund would be transferred to the equity market.

The second proposal was called the Individual Accounts plan (IA).

This would cut benefits for those on higher incomes and again increase payroll taxes by a small amount. This increase in payroll taxes would go towards an individual defined-contribution savings account. These accounts would be invested by a mutual fund which would be managed by the government.

The third proposal was known as the Personal Security Account plan (PSA). This would introduce a two-tiered arrangement in the social security system. The first tier would provide a universal flat-rate benefit. The second tier would provide a mandatory personal retirement account financed by an increase in the payroll tax, but the increase would be higher than in the other two proposals. The funds arising from this increase would then be invested by a private investment institution as directed by the individuals participating in the plan.

All three proposals therefore introduced some reliance on the private sector and an increase in private investment of one sort or another using private accounts. In 1999, the Clinton administration went even further in proposing a major privatisation of social security through the investment of a major part of the accumulated public funds on the stock market, especially in equities. This produced an interesting contradiction. It set those who wanted to privatise but preserve government involvement against those who also did, but who at the same time did not want the government to retain an interest in what subsequently happened to investments – the 'backdoor to nationalisation' as described by the World Bank and separately by Martin Feldstein, to which I referred earlier.

Alan Greenspan, the Chairman of the US Federal Reserve, launched a more sophisticated criticism of the Clinton proposal, again demonstrating the gaps in the case put forward by some of the privatisers; even if the arguments were directed more against the role of the state and the dangers of political interference which he had earlier stated. He argued that the process of moving $600 billion of public funds from bonds into equities would raise the price of equities and therefore lower their rate of return. Any increases from equities would be offset by lower returns in the rest of the economy, in particular reductions in returns from private portfolios which represented savings for retirement (*Financial Times,* 1999c, p. 6). This assumes what I shall call a steady state of economic assets in which there is no new production as a result of the increased investment in equities – a neat rejection of the World Bank and Feldstein case, which appeared to assume that an increase in supply creates its own demand and will thereby increase the 'capital stock' and rates of return.

So privatisers faced an interesting conundrum posed by the desire to address the issue of public expenditure on the one hand and by the need to explain how they would increase rather than depress the aggregate rate of return on the other. This was something which had once appeared quite straightforward.

In any case, many proposals by reformers depend, broadly speaking, on making further cuts to social security and raising the retirement age. After that, the resultant savings would be used for a mandatory private pension plan which would be invested on the market. The fiscal implications of larger private provision with the attendant tax concessions are usually ignored in the calculation of future 'liabilities'. The broader fiscal implications of the use of the funds through the stock market for productive investment do not usually enter the equation of the reform movement.

However, the battle for reform continued. The first report from the social security trustees in the year 2000 predicted a deficit of $21.6 trillion between 2015 and 2075. Other arguments suggested that social security would be able to pay for all benefits for the following thirty-seven years, even based upon assumptions of economic growth over seventy-five years which were about half the rate for the previous seventy-five years. The possible shortfall advocated by some critics of existing arrangements, and the pessimistic forecasts by others for the subsequent seventy-five years, implied increases in public budget commitments of less than 1 per cent of national income over the period, others argued.

Both the Democratic and Republican presidential candidates in

2000 favoured some further private solution to the alleged crisis in social security. Governor Bush proposed individual social security investment accounts in which savers could invest a part of their social security contributions. Vice-President Gore pledged to 'save' social security, proposed a new form of retirement savings plan similar to the 401(k) accounts. This seemed to confirm the bi-partisan approach to privatisation which has emerged in the reformist approaches. The same applies to the UK.

THE UK

In the UK, there have been many proposals to encourage greater coverage of earnings-related pensions, but improvements to the basic pension and the State Earnings-Related Pension Scheme (SERPS) are rarely suggested. The Commission on Social Justice, set up by the Labour Party leader, and the Commission on Wealth Creation, set up by the Liberal Party leader, both included senior academics as well as politicians and practitioners of various social and corporate activities. The former considered improvements to SERPS as an option but pointed out many weaknesses in the scheme. The latter wanted to increase long-term investment. They both contained recommendations on pension reform which promoted funding (Commission on Social Justice, 1994; Commission on Wealth Creation, 1995).

The debates continued through the 1990s with improvements to the basic pension and to SERPS becoming increasingly unlikely. The arguments and proposals of Jane Falkingham and Paul Johnson provide a further example of the tone and the parameters of discussions about pension reform. Falkingham and Johnson identified the two main problems which recent reports and enquiries had addressed: the ageing of the population and the fact that a substantial proportion of the population does not have the income to accumulate large private pensions. They then proposed a personal pension system which, they argued, would avoid the problems of the personal pension sector by licensing only a small number of 'established financial institutions'. A person whose contributions were too low to provide a minimum pension would receive an annual top-up from the state, either to be repaid when income allowed, or to be converted into a grant or subsidy if not. This 'United Funded Pension System', as the authors called it, also relied on investing the contributions, including the grants from the state. They both asked:

> Can the left ditch its emotional commitment to a national insurance system and a basic pension that can no longer perform at even a minimum level of adequacy? Can New Labour 'think the unthinkable' and form an alliance with the major financial institutions to develop a radically different pension system for Britain in the twenty-first century?
>
> (Falkingham and Johnson, 1996, p. 167)

The proposal certainly tried to target the worst-off. But 'think the unthinkable'? They did not explain what was supposedly 'unthinkable' about working with the private sector. Even 'Old Labour' promoted the initial compromise with financial institutions in the 1970s which laid the basis for the UK's contribution to what became the Anglo-American model (Minns, 1980 and 1997).

In this proposal, it is not really clear why the commitment to national insurance should be, emotively, 'ditched' in favour of yet more private-sector provision. Unfortunately, 'established financial institutions' were also subject to enquiry and financial penalties for the mis-selling of personal pensions in the 1980s, a policy which, as we have noted, incurred great cost for the public Exchequer. Perhaps the authors acknowledge some of these problems with financial institutions. But these firms were not 'unestablished' financial institutions. They were not some pension bucket shops operating out of someone's back room or garage. They included the Prudential Assurance Company and Lloyds and Midland Banks with their prestigious histories.

In a nutshell also, most reformers rely by and large on the conventional structures of financial institutions and capital markets, and ignore the effects on investment and production. Both the Conservative and Labour governments of the 1990s proposed an extension of private provision through various approaches to extending personal pension provision with pensions related to ability to contribute and on the vagaries of the stock market. The Conservative proposals contained the larger shift to further private provision, effectively phasing out the state basic and earnings-related pensions. While still offering a state guarantee, the basis of all pension provision in practice would be provided by the market. The Labour proposals were aimed at providing market-based personal pensions (stakeholder pensions) to low- and middle-income groups.

The role of the state was marginalised in all the major reformist proposals of the 1990s.

THE 'NEW RISK CULTURE' LOBBY

Let us next examine the claims of various other reformers and interest groups that, putting all else to one side, a capital-market-based pension system will have fundamental effects on the economic 'culture', on economic growth and on 'rates of return'. Here we come clearly into the realm of pensions and their role in the structure of financial systems and investment in production.

The European Federation for Retirement Provision, a lobby group dominated by British and Dutch funded pensions interest groups, in a European Commission Green Paper, summed up the case for privatisation. It stressed the beneficial effects of privately funded and invested pension funds for the development of European capital markets (EFRP, 1996). It further proposed that there should be a target of 25 per cent of pension payments in Europe which would come from funded pension arrangements, compared with 7 per cent at the time, and coverage of 60 per cent as opposed to 23 per cent. This would increase the funds from $1,270 billion to $12,700 billion by 2020.

This asset-expansion would improve liquidity and lower capital costs, it argued, and provide a large pool of risk capital arising from the alleged long-term investment horizon of pension funds. It would improve the 'equity culture' in continental Europe, making continental European investors less risk-averse. Naturally, this improved situation for capital-market development and supposed greater risk-taking could only occur if pension funds received improved tax status – the new risk culture has to be subsidised or underwritten by the offending dead hand of the state. This irony is lost on most of the participants and advocates in the discussions.

This concept of increasing risk-taking is interesting and demonstrates the innate confusion of the 'privatisers' about the role of capital markets in the economy. Capital markets, in fact, are supposed to do the opposite of what is claimed by the European Federation and many others. They are supposed to *reduce* risk, not increase it. They are intended to enable investors to 'hedge' against risk by increasing 'liquidity' – the maximisation of shorter-term gains and the ability to buy and sell without commitment to particular lines of business investment. Commitment involves the sort of longer-term involvement in a project represented by alternative financial measures such as long-term loans.

This idea of a new 'risk culture' is, in practice, similar to the concept of flight capital discussed earlier – it is an analogous reaction to the problems of bank capital and lending, or of committing capital to specific long-term liabilities. The increase in liquidity – the ability to sell or exit – acts against the interests of long-term investment because it leads to attempts to out-guess the market rather than understanding the long-term productive capacity of companies or countries (Grabel, 1997). It is reactive rather than proactive.

The volatility introduced into the system, along with the ability to buy and sell companies and to try to second-guess governments, are clearly contrary to the theoretical underpinning of the capital-market model, whose advocates claim greater stability, longer-term investment and higher growth. But unfortunately, on the basis of the evidence about stability and growth which is related to stock-market-dominated economies, they are mistaken: there appears to be no correlation between economic growth and stock-market capitalisation as percentage of GDP.

Also, the apparent long-term nature of pension fund investment is often a reflection of the fact that investments are increasingly 'indexed' against the market – they copy market share movements in a passive, responsive manner. By the year 2000, for example, around one-fifth of the investment on the UK stock market was in 'index-tracker' funds – the passive buying and selling of shares in direct proportion to their weighting on the stock market. This is no indicator of 'long-term investment'. Instead, long-term investment, I suggest, implies some form of deliberate and conscious decision to make a commitment to specific projects. It does not mean that an investment takes place because of some self-imposed, but reactive and reflexive, strategy which provides an apparently easy exit route if required. Nor should it facilitate effortless capital gains from share disposals in the event of takeover bids in which investors need do nothing but follow the market and sell at the right time. It is illogical to argue for the promotion of liquidity *and* long-term commitment at the same time.

The capital-market business and its accompanying theory of risk culture has a compelling influence in many quarters. It is usually linked to arguments about improving rates of return. I now propose to examine this compelling issue of 'rates of return'. This is the ultimate defence of financial institutions and others against external 'interference' and is their measure of economic and social prosperity. The 'rate of return' is seen as some neutral arbiter of efficiency and resource allocation. It is supposedly 'neutral' because it is determined by the philosophy of individual choice, in which the organisation of finance and production, and the resultant rate of return, are dependent on the 'free' exercise of such individual choice. This is opposed to the reverse scenario – the determination of choice, risk and the rate of return by a very different organisation of finance and production.

6

Rates of Return and Welfare

If the new risk culture just discussed is not all it is made out to be, then there are also implications for the claims that the stock-market system will improve rates of return and thereby optimise national resources for the payment of pensions. There are various definitions of 'rates of return' which we need to identify in order to examine more fully the logic of the Anglo-American theory and its empirical evidence.

RETURNS ON 'ASSETS'

The stock-market theory is based on property/asset-ownership and the financial return on those assets. This structure and philosophy is simply unable to take into account the broader social implications of this economic activity. Its objective, I would maintain, is to maximise financial returns on specific pieces of property or 'assets'. These returns on specific assets are alleged to be the basic criterion for the allocation of capital and the subsequent creation of economic growth.

In terms of the impact on pensions, if the financial returns and profits are dependent on employment cuts and unproductive corporate takeovers, for example, the 'return' may look 'better', but, simply put, this reduces the 'capital stock' and also reduces the ability of those affected by cuts to produce the required savings. It makes pensions 'reforms' even more dependent on support from the offending state, thus aggravating the pressures for shifting even greater responsibility from the 'bloated' state to the unproductive stock market.

Why unproductive, and why a reduction in the capital stock?

Let us consider the following. During the period 1982–95 only about 2 per cent of all UK stock-market turnover went towards the provision of new capital to companies. Of that, a substantial amount was devoted to takeovers, repayment of debt and the financing of dividends, an argument to which I will return in more detail in Chapter 8 (for earlier work, see Martin and Minns, 1995). A tiny amount went towards what the stock-market theorists, such as Feldstein (1997a, pp. 25 ff), optimistically call 'productive capital stock' or 'business plant and equipment'.

In addition, the history of takeovers in the UK, for example, has not produced increased productivity of capital or corporate expansion. New issues on the stock market also include privatisation of state-owned industry and the 'demutualisation' of insurance companies and building societies – the latter actually handing substantial sums *back* to savers, either in the form of free or discounted shares, or as straight cash. Indeed, Colin Mayer (1988) found that, between 1970 and 1985, in the UK and the US, new issues actually made a negative contribution to investment – there were net redemptions of stocks due to takeovers and mergers and the consequent buying of stock by acquiring companies. For the US, Robert Wade and Frank Veneroso also found that net savings transferred to the corporate sector through the equity market averaged less than 1 per cent of GDP over the decade to 1998, and were often negative (Wade and Veneroso, 1998). Doug Henwood calculates that between 1981 and 1997, US non-financial corporations paid back $813 billion more in stock than they issued, due to takeovers and buybacks (Henwood, 1998, p. 3). Ajit Singh also quotes data which show that between 1970 and 1989, the contribution of equity markets to the investment requirements of the corporate sector in the US and the UK was negative (Singh, 1996). His review of the literature shows no correlation between stock-market development and economic growth.

But these are developed economies. What about developing economies, where the capital market may be more 'primary', that is, less 'mature' and less dominated by 'secondary' transactions of existing shares? Their capital markets could therefore hypothetically be more useful in supporting and funding economic growth.

Pension funds are indeed involved in emerging markets. A survey in 1996 of sixty-five major US pension funds reported that the average portfolio allocation to these markets was 3.75 per cent of assets, with one-quarter of them expecting to increase the level of exposure by an average of 50 per cent over the following six to twenty-four months. Another, much larger survey found that the figure was 1 per cent – a more extensive review of funds of different size producing, not surprisingly, a lower figure. In the UK, a survey of over 700 pension funds reported a figure of 1.3 per cent of total assets at mid-1995 (IFC, 1996). Pension funds in Japan and Chile were also allowed to invest in emerging markets in 1995.

The World Bank puts the total pension fund assets in emerging markets at $70 billion for 1996–97 (World Bank, 1997a, p. 21). Emerging-market capitalisation at the time was 9 per cent of the world total. This would in turn give pension funds between 3.5 and 4 per cent of the total of emerging markets. If we add in estimates for insurance company-run personal pensions in the UK, and 401(k) pension plans run by the mutual funds in the US, then a conservative estimate would put the figure for foreign pension-related investment at around 6 per cent of total market value in these areas.

Unfortunately the evidence here is not encouraging for confirming the capital market as the engine of growth. Instead, privatisation programmes appear to have played a very important role in driving stock-market development – sales of government companies have consumed the domestic and foreign investment while, at the same time, increasing the size of the markets. In Chile, in 1990, holdings in privatised companies accounted for 90 per cent of all the equity holdings of pension funds (Fischer, 1998).

Rather than providing new capital for productive investment in these economies, the equity market has functioned as a facilitator of ownership transfers. In addition, the international debt crisis of the 1970s encouraged the development of local stock markets in order to attract non-debt foreign investment to replace debt burdens. Nationalised industries in these economies have also been encouraged to use private markets rather than borrowing from the state. Some countries have also placed limits on debt/equity ratios in bank-based systems in order to encourage the use of equity rather than bank debt (Singh, 1996; Singh, 1995; Pfefferman, 1988).

This has tended to switch the sources of investment rather than necessarily increase the overall amount. The contribution of the stock market to economic growth in developing economies may have increased, but only by replacing non-stock-market sources of capital. The extent of the contribution by pension funds, through the equity markets, to the creation of new investment and productive activity is thereby, again, highly arguable.

One interesting example of how stock markets *could* work is provided by the Provident Fund in Malaysia. Like the Singapore Provident Fund, the Malaysian Employees Provident Fund was established in the early 1950s and is a statutory body operating under the Ministry of Finance. Investment 'deregulation' in 1991 and 1995 lowered its proportion of required investment in government securities and, consequently, its investment in money markets, bonds and equities increased. Prior to that, the fund, according to the World Bank, assisted in infrastructure investment indirectly by investing in government securities, helping the development of the Kuala Lumpur airport, the light rail transit system and the important north–south expressway. The government reportedly intended to list some of these infrastructure projects on the local stockexchange which would provide, in stock-exchange parlance, a boost for the fund's equity investments in these projects and provide an opportunity for realising capital gains (World

Bank, 1997b, proposing the standard pension-fund reforms for China, p. 59). This is, however, an interesting example of the real value of a market in investments which *could* finance productive activity if the orientation of the market were different.

To return to the reality of financial markets more generally, the stock-market theory equates economic success (using GDP as the measure) with financial rates of return on specific assets, along with 'cost'-reduction. Higher rates of return must indicate greater growth. Unfortunately, even in its own stock-market terms, there is no correlation between returns on share investments and GDP growth.

For example, comparing the US, the UK, Japan, Australia, Canada and Germany over the ten-year period 1984–93 inclusive, the UK had the highest returns in its equity market, but the lowest increase in GDP. The same applies for the twenty-five years from 1966 to 1990 inclusive for the UK compared to Australia, Canada, Denmark, Germany, Japan, Netherlands and the US (Willmore, 1998). There is also no connection between *size* of equity market, equity returns and economic growth.

Sometimes, of course, the results of these analyses depend on the timescale or groups of years which are chosen for comparison. But such selectivity cannot conceal the overall difference between GDP growth and stock-market returns.

Finally, when looking at the rankings of the countries of the world in terms of GDP per head, the US, at number nine in the league table of highest rates, has five of the countries from the European bloc (as represented in Table 2) ahead of it. The UK, the other core Anglo-American country, listed at number twenty-two in the league table, has eleven ahead of it.

In other words, it is difficult to equate the countries which have small equity markets and lower levels of funded pension arrangements to 'protect the old', on the one hand, with a failure to 'promote growth', on the other (to use the optimistic key words from the subtitle of the 1994 World Bank report).

Let us now consider this broader issue of returns.

ECONOMIC AND SOCIAL RETURNS

Following on from the previous arguments, I suggest that there is a built-in contradiction in the stock-market theory. Economic welfare or 'returns', or even economic growth, are not necessarily the same as the rate of return on specific assets. Financial returns do not appear to be a surrogate for economic or social health. And the more we add to these markets in financial returns, the greater the apparent contradiction, and the more their ability to ignore, or not connect with, broader economic and social returns. Without employment, for example, people cannot make the savings on which the whole theory is based. They rely on the safety net, thus fuelling allegations that the system is too costly and should be replaced by more private (and normally, of course, publicly subsidised) provision. But what happens when broader considerations of economic and social welfare are taken into account by pension-fund investors?

One survey of research in the US referred to figures showing funds with 'politically minded' investments under-performing their 'benchmarks', while those without such investments did slightly better than their benchmarks. It described the particular case of Connecticut's state pension fund in 1990 investing $25 million in Colt Firearms to keep 925 local jobs which appeared to be under threat. After two years, Colt filed for bankruptcy and the investment was apparently lost (Morgenson, 1999).

Similarly, 'economically targeted investments (ETIs)' come under attack for producing lower rates of return in a CATO Institute publication (Lips, 1999). Commenting on the fact that the total assets of state and local retirement systems in the US amounted to just over $2 trillion (a huge proportion of world pension assets), it raised concerns about investments which were not in conformity with standard portfolio investment criteria. A number of instances are cited and reports referred to, including a Pennsylvania retirement fund which invested in a $70 million Volkswagen plant which, allegedly, lost 57 per cent of its value over fourteen years.

These figures and anecdotes take no account of the broader social

returns, which indeed are a complex issue. I wonder what fiscal benefit the state of Connecticut gained from the tax revenues received from
one large company and 925 people in employment during the period
described in the Morgenson article. What was the effect registered by
the new litmus test of economic growth? Following closure, what was
the subsequent cost of unemployment to the same state of
Connecticut? What was the cost of lost consumer spending for local
retailers, lost orders for suppliers and perhaps further, knock-on effects
from associated bankruptcies or lay-offs and lost revenues?

The same applies to the investment in the Volkswagen plant in terms
of tax revenues and multiplier effects (over fourteen years, no less).
Along with this we should take into account the financial cost to the tax-
payer of doing nothing for local investment. The consequences for local
demand for labour, goods and services could be substantial. Perhaps
these factors enabled hundreds or thousands of other people to continue
paying into their pension systems, thereby propping up an inherently vulnerable structure dependent upon the vagaries of stock-market returns.

Nevertheless, the CATO publication quotes a Congressional Report
on ETIs which presents a not untypical view of the impending apoca-
lypse which could be triggered by meddling with the measurement of
returns as determined by the 'market'.

Although the evidence presented above has dangerous implications for
America's pension system, there are consequences beyond just pension
plans. According to standard economic theory, optimal economic growth
requires the efficient use of all resources, including capital. If capital is
diverted to less productive uses, economic growth will be slower than it
would be otherwise . . . The potential for ETIs to harm the nation's economic growth is considerable: by forcing pension funds to finance less
productive investments, the economy will suffer. The long run slowdown of
economic growth caused by the ETI-induced misallocation of capital will
depress income growth and the standard of living.
(Joint Economic Committee House Staff Report, 'The Economics of ETIs:
Sacrificing Returns for Political Goals', September 1995)
(Lips, 1999, pp. 5–6)

The language used in the quotation and the title of the report is instructive. 'Dangerous implications', 'less productive', 'misallocation of capital', 'sacrificing returns for political goals', 'forcing pension funds' are contrasted with financial returns and supposedly, objective, non-political financial rectitude. ETIs are elsewhere described as 'distortions', 'usually dreamed up by politicians rather than investment managers, that are designed to win votes and improve the lives of voters, not savers' (Littlewood, 1998, p. 70). The implication that investment managers are not 'political' underlines the alleged 'neutrality' or 'rationality' of market criteria and the associated theories which accompany it. Conversely, the implication that politicians should be non-political is also absurd.

The argument also suggests a conflict between savers and voters as if they were two different sets of people, the former having no votes and the latter having no savings. In other words, why politicians in a democracy should not act in the interest of voters (who also include savers) escapes me. And why the financial markets are somehow politically neutral is also naive and baffling. They have their own platform of public expenditure requirements or limitations, their own views about interest and exchange rates, their own assumptions about public ownership and the role of the public sector and trade unions. Perhaps the critics of current politics imply some other form of governmental regime – one determined, yet again, by the market: a market-ocracy or, more to the point, a finance-ocracy. But I digress.

The measure to be used for identifying 'optimal economic growth' is the supposedly neutral, non-'political' benchmark of financial return on a specific, isolated, individual investment. Financial return equals economic return and benefit, or is supposed to, according to the theory. This is related to the theory of 'rational expectations', usually discussed, and criticised, in the context of market volatility and the sub-optimising or irrational behaviour which is contained in manias, fads and bubbles (for instance, Kindleberger, 1996; Henwood, 1998).

If only 'standard economic theory' made such difficult investment choices so simple. We have already noted the lack of correlation between financial rates of return and economic growth. We will also consider below the financial crashes which can occur when investors follow each other in a mania guided by actual or prospective financial gain. As usual, the sin of commission (ETIs for instance) always provokes harsher assessments than the sin of omission (not joining the herd in the dash for the emerging, or 'submerging', markets). Whatever then happens when the bottom falls out of the particular fad, as measured by the guiding principle of financial rate of return, is ignored as markets allegedly 'recover'. The 'potential harm' to income growth and the standard of living created by relying solely on financial rate of return is not acknowledged, nor does it even enter the calculus. Whether the people affected by such collapses and 'recoveries' actually recover is another matter. But if the *markets* recover this is presented as an underlying ingredient of success or economic 'health'.

This is not to argue for the financing of anything that comes along in some frenzy of social expenditure and corruption of Keynesian demand-led economics. But, instead of dismissing everything which does not fit the narrow calculus of portfolio returns as 'politically minded' and thereby somehow (explicitly or implicitly) corrupt, there has to be a greater balance in our assessment, even in financial terms, of rates of return.

The economics of 'rates of return' has a complex political history, at least recently. In practical terms (academic work, business activity and politics), I have been on both sides of the argument. Of course, the balance is difficult, but it highlights the contradiction between financial rates of return and broader economic returns in terms of how we measure 'economic success' after the apparent collapse in 1989 of other measures of economic worth with the perceived fall of Communism. We need to adjust the hierarchy of 'returns' in order to examine who really gains from the present structure of investment and capital markets. My conclusion is that we simply have no adequate measure of 'rate of return'.

To push the argument further from one side of the divide, future pensioners can maximise their financial return by investing outside of their state or country if necessary while the economy is stagnant, the rate of taxation is increasing in order to pay for the rise in the unemployment 'dependency' ratio and the real standard of living falls. They may hope for a good pension, but, as I have mentioned, the production of local goods and services will have declined. They have a good rate of return perhaps in gross financial terms, but the net result is that they pay more tax. Maybe they also have to support their unemployed children, their streets are unsafe and many local facilities are closed.

Here, I introduce an addition to the litany of 'dependency ratios'. The 'international dependency ratio' will increase. This is a ratio of older people to the declining number of younger productive workers based in other countries who can produce the goods and revenue to support them. This international dependency ratio could encourage a new kind of 'rentier' economy. At the risk of becoming a bit fanciful, this economy would be dependent on a supply or importation of out-of-state or foreign goods and services, paid for by returns on out-of-state or foreign financial assets. However, if the Anglo-American model has taken root extensively elsewhere, there is a limit to how far a declining part of the world can support the spread of the rentier economy. There is a limit to how far the international dependency ratio is sustainable.

In the meantime, it could provide good business for the European model, I suppose. In this fanciful model, countries with a European-type system increase their supplies and exports to the Anglo-American rentier world. But, then, this would be self-defeating. It would be dependent on massive investment into Europe by the Anglo-American pension funds in order to produce the necessary returns and income to pay for the imports. It would thereby add to the tendency, which we have already noted, of the European financial model moving towards the more unproductive Anglo-American structure of finance and welfare. This structure emphasises capital gains for shareholders from such activities as takeovers and mergers as opposed to real increases in production.

Let us consider this issue further. In the calculus of stock-market

returns, no assessment is made of the overall economic cost of the substantial unproductive takeovers and mergers which may make huge
capital gains for investors in the stock-market model, but which appear
to do little for economic growth. There is now considerable evidence
which demonstrates the limited or negative impact of such activity,
along with arguments that it leads to a short-term view on the part of
portfolio investors (some referred to by Singh, 1996, and Singh and
Weisse, 1998). I shall return to this in more detail when we consider
the effect of portfolio investment on economic growth in 'emerging
markets'.

Thus, it is not the cost of ageing populations and their inability to
save because of low or interrupted employment that are the problems. The problem is the role of portfolio investment and financial
markets themselves in the creation of that low or interrupted employment. All the proposals for pensions improvement take everything in
the market as given. They attempt to adjust benefits and contributions around it and the measure of return is corrupted by a financial
index which appears to be irrelevant for the assessment of the real
standard of living.

Social expenditure has got shunted into a financial dead-end
concerned with cost or profit. The main issue about employment/
production and the unproductive stock market is ignored.

RETURNS FROM 'PYRAMID SELLING'

A related argument is this. The stock-market theory implies something for nothing – that it will create more value or 'growth' through
its self-expansion, and therefore give capital and labour a greater ability to meet all their expectations. However, as we have mentioned,
pension funds (funded schemes) are seen by many as 'deferred
wages'.[9] Their origins have been substantially influenced by labour
agreements (in particular in the US, the UK and Australia) to curb
current wages. In other words, labour, by reducing wage claims, agreed

that capital could retain a greater part of the surplus in exchange for a paper claim on that surplus to be redeemed in the future by labour. It is a paper claim because, as I have implied in my argument, it reflects a purchase of securities from someone else and is not necessarily equivalent to a net increase in real assets or economic development. This underlines Bernard Friot's arguments about the problematic nature of the concept of *deferred* wages when, instead, we should be considering wages and pensions as the same thing, earned by *current* production (Friot, 1997). The former creates a bi-polar view of welfare, the latter sees it as a totality.

What then happens in the future when the beneficiaries want to realise their claims? If the growth in the world's accumulated capital assets exceeds the increase in real growth – as it has done in the US and the UK, and as we have seen in world markets in 1998 – then investment will run into rapidly diminishing returns. In technical terms this means a collapse of price–earnings ratios, thereby causing a collapse in share values and enormous capital losses. But, surely, if people nevertheless get better pensions from stock markets, then the switch to greater private provision must have done the trick? Unfortunately, even in good times, if stock-market returns have nothing to do with real growth, then security in retirement is an illusion. Pensioners can only share in what is produced when they are, in fact, pensioners (unless they store up twenty years' worth of tinned food and dried milk beforehand). If production has fallen, their savings buy less in real terms. 'Diversification' of risk by investing in overseas stock markets (UK pension assets are at least 30 per cent based outside the country) does not square the circle either, as we have seen with the international financial crisis and all its knock-on effects.

What then are the savings going to be worth if they have expanded without any equivalent in the real economy, nationally and internationally? Even before the stock-market crises of 1997–98, pension assets were valued at more than the worth of *all* the companies quoted on the world's three largest stock markets – the US, the UK and Japan.

If it cannot be put to productive use then stock-market investment rapidly hits diminishing returns. Indeed, this is reminiscent of arguments in classical economics about 'oversaving' in earlier versions of 'supply-side economics' (summarised in Fairmount, 1996, Chapter 4), an issue which we have also touched on earlier in our discussion of savings and investment. In some of the arguments of classical economics, saving was endorsed as beneficial *per se*. But, some argued, where could savings go if domestic investment opportunities were not increasing? In this approach, international investment was encouraged because it raised the rate of return on domestic investment. If the investments were restricted to the home economy, returns would decline as opportunities were exhausted. A new demand could be created by investing in higher-risk, higher-return investments overseas, and this would thereby stabilise or increase the domestic rate of return. Higher returns elsewhere based on cheaper production costs would put pressure on wages at home and thereby increase the share of wealth accruing to capital. When we consider international financial crises later we will see some of the negative consequences of this. Even ignoring financial crises, however, the OECD argues that the outcome in any case will only lead to the equalisation of returns (OECD, 1998b) and the funds will be back where they started. We are still left with the issue of the relationship between the growth of savings and growth in the real economy.

In an earlier chapter we have also seen the high ratios of stock-market valuations to GDP in some individual countries, especially the US and the UK. By the last quarter of 1999, US stock markets rose to an unprecedented 140 per cent of GDP, leading to warnings by the Federal Reserve and predictions of economic deflation. Whatever the ultimate resolution of the imbalance between stock valuations and the real economy, the risk of something going wrong in the meantime is worth considering. In 1997–98 fifteen Japanese funds, including the large rice-dealers' scheme, collapsed. 'They could only survive when economy and stock markets were booming' (*Financial Times*, 1998f). *The funds depend on the economy, not the other way around.*

The OECD warned that a 20 per cent decline in overvalued stock markets around the world could reduce the economic growth of 1.7 per cent which has been predicted for the industrialised world to around 1 per cent. It stated in 1998 that stock markets were highly overvalued by historical standards, increasing the risk that share prices could crash again. If the bubble of overpriced equities bursts, consumer confidence would be hit as the value of pensions and other investments declines, in turn leading to a slowdown in growth (report by Charlotte Denny of a presentation by the acting head of the OECD's economic policy studies department of their biannual economic outlook, in the *Guardian*, 1998, p. 25). By the year 2000, the Bank of International Settlements warned about the implications of soaring asset markets and asserted that the current stock-market valuations were unlikely to be sustainable in the long term (*Financial Times*, 2000b, p. 1).

The ultimate conundrum is therefore this. When the current generation of hopeful savers retires, their savings schemes must attract more savers to keep the system going and pay the pensions – the claims on the underlying assets, the shares in companies, the property holdings and government securities must be sold to other savers, or these schemes too will get into difficulty. But if global economic growth does not match the growth in pension claims on rising stock markets, those claims will be worth less than the share of the surplus being supposedly 'deferred' (and which, incidentally, could have been transferred to current, poorer pensioners). The way we pay for welfare or social security may indeed have added to the supply side of capital flows (pension savings) rather than the demand side (government expenditure), but eventually the supply must convert into demand, even in general terms, thus creating the 'pension pyramids' where the whole structure depends on a continual supply of funds to pay off earlier creditors and contributors. The risk, in the meantime, of being caught by the collapse of some investment fad, causing panic and crash, cannot be easily ignored.

This may sound melodramatic, and I understand that such a crisis may result from other causes – that pension funds may not be so speculative as to be the proximate cause of a price collapse of such proportions. Nevertheless the underlying implications of the trend should be of some concern. As Kindleberger has argued, the trigger for a panic and crash can be quite arbitrary, but the consequences of the crash for those who do not get out at the top of the market (many, by definition, will not) can be devastating (Kindleberger, 1996). In this context, as Henwood has cannily observed, the privatisation of social security in the US – transferring huge sums of money from the public Exchequer to the stock markets as proposed by the Clinton administration, to which we referred earlier – could constitute an enormous, even unprecedented, official stock-price support mechanism (Henwood, 1998, p. 7).

Following this, there is one final, and very important application of the 'rate of return' concept I want to consider.

RETURNS ON PAY-AS-YOU-GO

The central issue about the application of balance sheet accountancy standards to macroeconomic and social questions of welfare is underlined in another concept – the rate of return on pay-as-you-go schemes.

The predicted poor 'returns' on pay-as-you-go schemes are allegedly aggravated by demographic forecasts. This means that, as the proportion of workers to pensioners falls – in other words, as the system 'matures' – then the rate of return on contributions falls. Workers are paying in relatively more than a previous generation did in order to receive the same pension in real terms. The first generation in the scheme probably only paid in for part of their working lives when the system was beginning, but they nevertheless received the full pension – a 'good rate of return'. By definition the later generation receives a lower 'rate of return', and if the old-age dependency ratio worsens, then they will be even worse off in terms of the 'return' on their expenditure – what they 'paid in'.

Whether their 'return' amounts to a reasonable income seems irrelevant in this personalised calculus of contributions, entitlements and percentages. Instead, it is argued, if they had invested on stock markets they would have received a higher percentage rate of return and not suffered from the lower returns resulting from the maturing of the pay-as-you-go scheme. Tables of rates of return are produced to show the success of equity markets over GDP growth, turning to advantage the figures mentioned above which showed no link between financial returns and GDP growth. Equity markets may, after all, produce no growth, one infers, but they produce a better rate of return than pay-as-you-go.

But a rate of return for whom and from what? Where rates of return have beaten increases in GDP, especially in the UK for example, we should ask, what has been given up in terms of economic growth and investment by current and future generations in order to produce those rates of return? What are these rates of return based on?

Simple financial rates of return based on stock-market accounting criteria tell us nothing about who has benefited from them, who has paid for them, where they come from or how big is the asset base from which they have been generated. They may reflect nothing more than the rise in demand for stocks, bearing little relationship to the real economy, and may introduce a greater 'liquidity' and volatility into markets.

As we have seen, demographic forecasts have been selective, stock-market returns do not equate with real economic returns and may be negative in the broader context. Funding apparent 'deficits' in pay-as-you-go schemes may be significantly less than thought because of this and may even be growth-enhancing, if that has to be a criterion.

Consider that the European Commission represents countries with a mixture of models, some of which have a strong flavour of inter-generational solidarity. The UK has had substantial political influence in these matters (in 1992, the EC Commissioner responsible – Sir

Leon Brittan – tried to introduce a pensions directive which would 'liberalise' the management and investment of European pension schemes). However, by 1997, while seeking 'reforms' in order to avoid budget deficits 'crowding out expenditure on social protection', and bowing to the UK lobby on 'freedom of capital movements', the EC decided not to advocate the extension of funded schemes. Interestingly, it used the same theme about the dependency of welfare on economic growth, but from the opposite viewpoint. Pay-as-you-go, according to this view, is a component of economic growth and social cohesion (CEC, 1997, para. 1.2). The idea of such a directive resurfaced in 2000, but there was considerable criticism from the privatisation lobby that it contained such potential 'opt-outs' – a favourite tool of UK diplomacy in the EU – that it would not have much effect on the important French and German financial markets.

To continue their original political position, the EC also argued that current GDP is shared every year between those who receive income directly from their participation in economic life and those who do not. This applied to funded schemes as well as pay-as-you-go arrangements. In other words, funding does not isolate a part of current national income for unspecified future use, with interest, by those who defer their consumption. As we have noted earlier, future pensioners depend, like everyone else, on what the economy is capable of producing at the time, and at what price. In other words, the debate apparently hides a conflict about the division of *current* national income.

An interesting dimension to this has been added by Mary Campbell in her examination of the UK pension system. Her analysis has significant implications for the rate of return on public pensions and the division of national income.

First, the UK state pension is not more expensive than private pensions – the rate of return is not lower. The annual cost of the state pension is the gross outgoing from the National Insurance Fund, not the net cost to the Exchequer. Because there is a contributory element, it is likely that the state pension actually makes a net contribution to the Exchequer – there is not a negative effect on the rate of return for the national budget.

Second, and most important from our point of view here, the state pension is subjected to the tax system, thereby lowering the rate of return for individuals in comparison to private arrangements. Contributions to state pensions are not tax-deductible, unlike private pensions. These arrangements penalise the worst-off, for whom the state pension is much more important. The fact that the state pension itself is also taxable makes it unique in thereby being taxed twice. Moreover, tax relief on private pension arrangements is at the marginal rate, meaning that the people in higher tax-brackets benefit more. Similarly, a large part of the private pension can be received as a tax-free lump sum (Campbell, 1998).

Bryn Davies has discussed some of these distributional issues in relation to equity between different generations in the structure of pension systems.

> Debates on the intergenerational effects of different pension systems often involve information about the rate of return achieved on the contributions paid by and on behalf of participants . . . The results usually show younger cohorts of participants in pay-as-you-go systems do significantly worse than those who are in at the beginning of such system.
>
> (Davies, 2000, p. 117)

The problem is the validity of such arguments when applied to pension systems which are based on the concept of solidarity. Are these arguments any more valid, Davies asks, than asking what rate of return is achieved when we pay for health services?

> The returns on these elements of taxation or social security contributions are partly objective, expressed in cash terms, but also subjective, expressed both in terms of offering reassurance for the individual and in feelings of solidarity with fellow citizens.
>
> (ibid., p. 117)

A telling example is this:

> it is possible, after the event, to show that people whose houses burn down get a better rate of return on their insurance premiums than those who are more lucky in this respect. This does not mean that it is sensible to suggest that the payment of the insurance premiums proved to be a bad decision. The point may be mathematically accurate, but it is irrelevant because it ignores the reason why the premiums were paid in the first place. They were not paid as an investment, they were paid to provide a feeling of security. In the same way the contributions paid to a pay-as-you-go pension system might be, at least in part, paid for reasons other than investment.
>
> (ibid., p. 117)

Furthermore the question of security could represent, in my view, a totally different concept of 'investment' and 'returns', to use the current methodology for the measurement of participation in society.

> It could well be argued that establishing a pension system where the current generation are treated well makes it more likely that future generations of pensioners will be treated in the same way, whatever the type of pension system.
>
> (ibid., p. 117)

Finally:

> The conclusion on the validity of using the rate of return to compare different pension systems is that while it can be done it is not the only relevant consideration to apply, let alone always the most relevant. In many cases it will be unimportant, particularly where a system has been established explicitly on a basis of intergenerational solidarity, where arguments based on the rate of return simply do not apply.
>
> (ibid., p. 118)

ECONOMIC EFFICIENCY AND SOCIAL CHOICES

Even among the economic experts, there are at least two diametrically opposed points of view about rates of return and related matters.

On the one hand, there are those who point to the improvements in savings, increases in the 'capital stock' (this 'elusive entity', to quote Arrighi, 1994), higher wages, private as opposed to state investment, lower cost of capital, higher rates of return and higher economic growth implied by the private model. In other words, they look to the greater all-round economic efficiency caused by the private provision of pensions through capital markets.

Again according to Feldstein, Professor of Economics at Harvard University and formerly Chairman of the Council of Economic Advisers under the Reagan administration:

> Responsible [whatever that implies for the others who have a different point of view] government officials have therefore concluded that the current system . . . cannot continue unchanged. The increased savings during working years that such a system of individual accounts entails, and the productivity of the resulting increased capital stock [again not defined], would permit future retirement and health care costs to be financed with much lower annual contributions than would be required under a pay-as-you-go system . . . It is difficult to think of *any other policy* that could produce such a substantial permanent rise in the standard of living of the vast majority of the population.
>
> (Feldstein, 1997a, pp. 25 and 38, my emphasis)

On the other hand, we have the view of Larry Willmore, an economist at the United Nations:

> Social security is increasingly debated in terms of alleged effects of public pensions on economic efficiency . . . the efficiency effects of such schemes are negligible. Social security reform in itself is not likely to generate increased savings or growth; it is essentially a zero sum game in which some participants gain at the expense of others. Arguments for reform of

social security masquerade as economics, while in reality they are political
arguments for changing the distribution of costs and benefits.

(Willmore, 1998, introductory abstract)

The poverty of the economic arguments about rates of return
underlines the real social choices. What economic evidence there is
does not confirm the privatisers' arguments. Adjusting the rate of
return on public pay-as-you-go is essentially a matter of social policy
and should be separated from arguments about the determinants of
economic growth and financial returns. It involves political choices,
not economic determinants.

The narrow definition of rate of return set by markets also has enormous implications for economic development more generally,
especially as applied to the supposed world of 'financial integration', as
countries, encouraged by the World Bank, set up and develop their capital markets and open their economies to financial 'intermediation'.

Let us now turn to some of the specific implications of this.

7

Manias, Panics and Pension Funds

More and more people now recognise the benefits of investment in real assets such as stocks and shares. While bank deposits are a sensible investment for short-term savings and as a source of emergency cash, in the medium to long term it is investments in real assets which have historically given greatest growth . . . [Our funds enable you] to share in the exciting and rewarding world of international financial markets.
(Scottish Provident International Life Assurance Ltd, Isle of Man, Capital Investment Portfolio, 1998–99 Prospectus, p. 3)

We will now consider some of the broader implications of pension fund financial flows, revisiting earlier comments on the international implications of private pension fund investment. Pension funds provide an important insight into the causes of international financial crises, especially as they have fed the 'mania' of the 1990s for diversification into the so-called growth stocks of emerging markets. Charles Kindleberger has written about financial manias, panics and crashes (Kindleberger, 1996). So more recently has Charles Morris, who has also made some reference to pension funds in his analysis, mainly of financial crises and crashes in the US (Morris, 1999).

I now want to indicate more fully the role of pension funds in some of the latest manias and panics.

FINANCIAL FLOWS TO DEVELOPING COUNTRIES

'Emerging markets' of interest to institutional investors grew significantly over the ten years to 1998. There are 166 'developing countries'
referred to by the World Bank, a group of which constitute the
International Finance Corporation (IFC) Emerging Markets Index
(IFCI) (World Bank, 1997a, pp. 11 and 15). Reflecting the fluidity of
the situation, sometimes the words 'developing countries' and 'emerging markets' are used interchangeably in official publications (IFC,
1998, p. 8, and World Bank, 1998, p. 3, use a similar table to portray
financial flows to 'emerging markets' in the former case and 'developing countries' in the latter).

Although institutional investors for the most part assess their investment policies for developing countries by using the IFCI smaller
group, the countries included in this index have nevertheless grown
over the ten years in which it has operated. This is a response to the
increase in the number of stock markets throughout the world (by
1997, seventy-five emerging markets were covered by the IFC reports –
IFC, 1998) and a growing interest among institutional investors themselves in a broader investment and geographical coverage (by 1997,
thirty-two countries were included in the IFCI, compared to eighteen
in 1996).

Bearing the differences of definition in mind, private capital flows
to 'developing countries' rose to $240 billion in 1996 (World Bank,
1997a, p. 9) and to $256 billion in 1997 (World Bank, 1998, p. 3)
from $33.3 billion in 1985. In 1985, official development finance
(funding through grants and loans from government and intergovernmental bodies) was higher than private flows. But by 1997, private
flows were nearly six times greater.

Table 6 summarises these figures. It also shows that foreign direct
investment (FDI) comprises the largest category of private flows. (FDI
includes corporate investment in overseas subsidiaries through the
increase in fixed capital investment, or the establishment or purchase of
ventures and plant, including the cross-border mergers and acquisitions

Table 6   Net Long-term Resource Flows to Developing Countries
(selected years; US $billion)

Type of Flow	1985	1990	1997
All Developing Countries	82.5	98.3	300.3
Official Development Finance	37.8	56.4	44.2
Total Private Finance	33.3	41.9	256.0
Debt flows	21.8	15.0	103.2
bank loans	8.5	3.8	41.1
bonds	5.6	0.1	53.8
other	7.6	11.1	8.3
Foreign Direct Investment	11.3	23.7	120.4
Portfolio equity	0.1	3.2	32.5
Official Development Finance as % of total flows	45.8	57.4	14.7
Equity, bonds as % of total	6.9	3.3	28.7
Equity as % of total	0.1	3.3	10.8

Source: adapted from IFC, 1998, p. 8; World Bank, 1998, p. 9.

that we have come across earlier). But portfolio flows (investment mainly in equities and bonds) rose ten times between 1990 and 1997, for example, while FDI rose five times. This is not to forget that, in so far as FDI originates largely from countries in the Anglo-American bloc, pension funds have an indirect role here as shareholders in the originating company.

By 1997, portfolio equity flows were similar to bank loans and official development finance in size. Moreover, total portfolio flows (bonds and equities) made up more than one-third of total private financial flows (World Bank, 1998, p. 9; IFC, 1998, p. 8; World Bank, 1997a, p. 11). But, 'Unlike FDI flows, portfolio flows to the emerging markets have been volatile' (IMF, 1997, p. 63) – a point to which we shall return below. By 1997 again, developing countries received

30 per cent of global portfolio capital, compared to only 2 per cent before 1990 (World Bank, 1997a, p. 15).

This international investment activity has increased substantially in geographical scope over only ten years, with greater 'financial integration' as defined by the World Bank (1997a), while, at the same time, the speed of reaction by international investors has also increased. The share of world stock-market capitalisation represented by emerging markets (the market value of securities on their stock markets) increased to 9 per cent of world capitalisation by 1997 (IFC, 1998, p. 18). This should be contrasted with just over 4 per cent in 1988. Despite ups and downs in the meantime, this growth is another indicator of the increase in the numbers of markets and the increase in investment in those markets, thereby enhancing their relative proportion of global stock-market capitalisation.

One of the major factors driving this growth has been the increase in the investment of pension funds and related institutional pension provisions, and their search for an increase in diversification of investments. The returns on investments in domestic markets are deemed to be flattening or they are predicted to reduce as the increase in private funds from ageing populations flows into a relatively fixed stock of tradable assets – a conundrum we came across earlier – thereby pushing prices up (a rise in stock-market indices in the US and the UK – the US Dow Jones and London 'FTSE' indices of stock-market prices). This is accompanied by a decline in relative income which can be received as a result of the rising cost of the assets on which the income relies. Emerging markets, however, appear as a way of buying low-priced assets in high-growth economies producing higher rates of return. There was deemed to be a low correlation between returns in developed markets and those in emerging markets. The increase in risk incurred by the investment in emerging markets is supposed to be at least equalised by the increase in the relative return.

As a result, pension funds held $70 billion of investments in emerging markets by 1997, representing around 1 per cent of their total assets (World Bank, 1997a, p. 22). In the US, pension funds held around 2 per cent of their total assets in emerging markets (3.75 per cent according to one source for 1996), while in the UK, surprisingly given the significantly higher proportion of total overseas holdings, the figure has hovered around 1 per cent, with the larger pension funds holding a larger percentage (IFC, 1996 and World Bank, 1997a for the US; for the UK, IFC, 1996, plus personal enquiries of UK pension funds and information from WM Company – UK performance measurement group).

What amounts to a small relative figure for the substantial pension funds of the developed markets has enormous implications for the smaller markets of the developing world. Indeed, what may be a small portfolio adjustment for one large institutional investor may have a major influence on an emerging market or markets, especially if other large institutions with their similarly small investments follow suit, as they seem to have done. In fact, 'The sheer size of institutional investor assets in the mature markets has meant that small changes in their portfolio allocations to emerging markets could have enormous effects on flows to those markets' (IMF, 1997, p. 88).

'FINANCIAL INTEGRATION'

One result of pension-fund and other institutional investment in emerging markets is said to be greater 'financial integration', a supposedly benign development which will help in the free flow of institutional finance throughout the world. Financial integration is measured by the World Bank (1997a) as comprising;

- access to international financial markets – as measured by 'country risk' ratings according to international risk assessment agencies;
- the ratio of private capital flows to GDP, with a higher weighting

given to portfolio investment and commercial bank lending (as opposed to FDI, for example);
• the diversification of a country's financing generally.

The top ten emerging markets in terms of financial integration for 1992–94 were: (1) Thailand, (2) Turkey, (3) Brazil, (4) Argentina, (5) Korea, (6) Indonesia, (7) Malaysia, (8) Mexico, (9) Hungary and (10) Ghana.

This list of the most integrated markets is particularly interesting in the light of the financial crises of 1997–99. The crises started with number 1 on the list, and subsequently spread to numbers 6, 7, 3, followed by the Philippines, number 13 of the total number of thirteen countries rated 'high' (compared to only two with such rating for 1985–87) on the scale of low, medium and highly integrated countries out of the sixty-five developing countries considered by the World Bank (World Bank, 1997a, pp. 17–18).

The 'push' factor for portfolio diversification is set to continue, it seems (IMF, 1997; OECD, 1998a). One argument is that if pension funds and mutual funds have between 1 and 2 per cent of their assets invested in emerging markets, then they are 'underweight' in emerging markets because, as noted above, the market capitalisation of those markets equals 9 per cent of total world market capitalisation. About 60 per cent of total world assets are outside the US, but the average US pension fund allocated only 16 per cent of its equity assets, and 8.8 per cent of total assets, to foreign stocks in 1995 (*Institutional Investor*, 1997, p. 106). Diversification, in other words, should allow for a closer matching of regional values within the global total.

In quantitative terms, relative to some other institutions, pension-fund investment in these markets will increase anyway because of the number of countries considering reforms to their state pension systems along Anglo-American lines, as we have discussed. This applies to all areas of the world. In Latin America the private-market response to pension reform exemplified by Chile in the early 1980s is being followed by reforms in Peru, Uruguay, Bolivia, Mexico, El Salvador,

Colombia and Argentina. In Central and Eastern Europe the process includes Hungary, Poland, Czech Republic, Latvia and Romania, among others.

Most important, however, are the continuing reforms in the developed world, including the possibility of the major privatisation of US social security pensions, and the extension of some form of additional private solutions in the UK – the two countries which dominate the world's league tables of private pension provision as measured by the size of pension funds and pension-related financial assets.

PROBLEMS WITH INCREASES IN EMERGING-MARKET INVESTMENT

The increase in assets may continue but the OECD points out that investment in emerging markets is not the solution to problems concerning the ageing population in the developed world (OECD, 1998b). Recall that this theory suggested that greater returns could be obtained from the emerging markets in order to offset the decline in returns in developed stock markets as a result of increasing demand causing rising prices from a fixed stock of assets. Through international diversification, future pensioners could thereby claim a greater share of world economic growth to compensate for the growing relative claim of ageing populations on more limited domestic economic growth.

Essentially, the contrary argument suggests that the overall returns will equalise or correlate as money leaves the low-return, high-asset-priced developed world and flows to the high-return, low-asset-priced developing world. Asset prices in the latter will go up and returns fall in relative terms, so levelling out the initial global variances. This even takes into account the downward pressure on returns relative to capital invested in developed markets as more people enter private plans for retirement savings invested on 'mature' or developed country stock markets. Indeed, the World Bank points out the inflationary implications of the increased demand for emerging market securities and views it as a negative local factor which should be countered by what remains of local economic policy discretion. We shall return to this point below.

Following another strand of argument, the World Bank argues that financial integration, as described above, can, however, promote better macroeconomic policies.

> Although integration increases the costs of policy mistakes in the short term, and increases the constraints on the conduct of macroeconomic policy, the market discipline that comes with integration can be a powerful force in promoting prudent and stable macroeconomic policies, with large benefits over the longer term. For instance, Indonesia's decision to open its capital account almost three decades ago has been an important element underpinning its track record of prudent and responsive economic policies.
>
> (World Bank, 1997a, p. 24)

These observations are somewhat unfortunate in the light of subsequent problems in 1997–98 for economies, like Indonesia's, which had introduced such open policies leading to greater financial integration. Indonesia was number 6 out of 65 on the World Bank list of integrated financial markets.

The advocates of greater portfolio flows acknowledge certain inherent risks. The first problem concerns 'surges' in private capital flows, with considerable variations between countries in the timing, magnitude and duration of the surges (World Bank, 1997a, p. 26). How do the surges arise?

The surge in flows in the 1990s initially reflected the 'strong economic performance' of the Asian countries, including rapid growth,

> sustained improvements in macroeconomic balances (public sector balances, inflation) and structural changes that have fostered a market-led, outward orientation since the late 1980s. The cyclical downturn in international interest rates in the early 1990s provided the initial impetus for the surge in flows (particularly portfolio flows); continued increases reflected

structural changes that have increased the responsiveness of capital to cross-border investment opportunities.

(World Bank, 1998, p. 31)

The surges are extremely large in relation to the size of the economies affected by them, with possible inflationary consequences. The World Bank lists twenty developing countries, half of which received annual inflows averaging more than 4 per cent of GDP during inflow episodes in the 1990s. Chile at a cumulative 25.8 per cent of GDP by the end of the inflow period, Malaysia at 45.8 per cent, Thailand at 51.5 per cent and Mexico at 27.1 per cent experienced the earliest and cumulatively the largest surges. South Asian countries experienced the surge after 1992, along with Eastern Europe, where the flows were very large. Low interest rates were a factor in these surges during 1990–93, but there were also changes in perceptions of creditworthiness. The consequent adjustments to institutional investment portfolios 'mean that surges in private capital are a likely feature of the early stages of integration' (World Bank, 1997a, p. 26).

The World Bank suggests that the next issue concerns the threat of major reversals of these flows. It notes that the reversal of flows in the case of Mexico triggered reversals in several other countries, notably in Argentina and Brazil. As well as the problem of major reversals, there are concerns about volatility and 'herding' in relation to private capital flows, especially the portfolio flows. Countries can become exposed to 'new sources of shocks' in the international economy and the effects of domestic shock can be magnified. This becomes even more important

because the degree of policy autonomy declines with growing financial integration . . . Investor herding and contagion effects may change investment in a country even if fundamentals are unchanged . . . Financial and capital markets in developing countries suffer more from incomplete and asymmetric information, and from other institutional weaknesses, than in industrial country markets. In this environment, the potential for investor

herding is greater, and domestic investors may be influenced by foreign
investors, leading to even greater volatility.

(World Bank, 1997a, pp. 27, 28 and 29)

Unlike foreign direct investment (FDI), 'portfolio investors can divest
themselves easily of their stocks of equities or bonds'. Moreover, while
volatility has tended to come down in the majority of countries, 'or at
least not increase . . . the absolute magnitude of variation is now much
greater, since the average level of flows is higher . . . Financial integration can therefore magnify shocks or the cost of policy mistakes,
leading to greater instability' (World Bank, 1997a, p. 143).

'Herding' is a result of problems arising from what is euphemisti-
cally described as 'asymmetric information', especially as the assets of
the primary investors – the pension funds or other originators of the
finance – are managed by 'professional fund managers' – banks and
other financial intermediaries. As a result, these fund managers will
follow the investment decisions of other fund managers in order to
show their pension fund and other clients that they know what they
are doing. If the investment goes wrong, they are more likely to be
judged as unlucky rather than incompetent, because others acted likewise. Given that such a large proportion of personal and pension-fund
assets is handled by these 'professional' managers, the World Bank
concludes that the potential for this behaviour 'clearly exists' (World
Bank, 1997a, pp. 126–7).

Even if domestic investors play a more significant and initiating
role in capital flight than some initially thought (IMF, 1998), the basic
issue remains. The enormity of the investment surges, herding and
contagion effects and the underlying growth in financial integration
(especially as measured by the index of stock-market turnover, which
includes all traders, domestic or not – a crucial measure in the World
Bank's assessment of integration), still represent the most significant
challenge to financial stability in emerging markets.

Indeed, the effects of financial integration are vitally important, as
domestic markets are drawn into a global market of financial flows

dwarfing the GDP of individual countries. All we have to do, in order fairly to allocate responsibilities in the explanation of crises, is to broaden the definition of flows to ensure that the role of domestic investors is appropriately acknowledged.

However, the question of who starts a flight of capital becomes increasingly academic. In the context of integrated financial markets and the enormity of financial flows, investment from the developed world in particular, through increasing pressures to privatise the 'burden' of ageing populations, will dominate the sources of stock-market turnover in developing countries for many years to come.

THE RISK OF FINANCIAL INSTITUTIONS THEMSELVES

There are two other factors to consider in the assessment of instability in financial markets, in which pension funds and pension-related investment play a crucial part.

Financial innovation and technical capacity have produced a significant range of new financial instruments and vehicles, especially the financial derivatives (including 'swaps', 'forwards', 'options' for foreign exchange, interest rates, equities and commodities) and hedge funds (private investment partnerships and offshore funds with wide flexibility to invest in securities and derivatives, and with wide powers to 'leverage', or borrow against their assets). These can change the risk profile of investment institutions very quickly. The growth of the global derivatives markets has been phenomenal (IMF, 1997, p. 120). When we also consider the concentration of investment management in relatively few organisations, along with the combinations of different financial activities within one particular institution or financial conglomerate and the connections between the institutions, then a further issue concerning risk appears.

We have noted earlier the concentration of investment activity in the hands of relatively few institutions. The IMF itself points out that in the US the ten largest institutional investors managed assets of

$2.4 trillion in 1995 (IMF, 1997, p. 120). This is exactly 10 per cent of all the financial assets of institutional investors within the OECD area according to OECD data for total assets for the same year. The IMF further adds that it is widely held that there will be considerably more concentration through consolidation in the fund-management business as well as geographically. This could give rise to the scenario of 'a relatively small number of very large global companies each managing assets well in excess of $150 billion and a number of smaller management companies surviving in regional niche markets' (IMF, 1997, p. 121). By 1998, a mere twenty financial institutions individually managed assets in excess of the $150 billion benchmark – with cumulative total assets amounting to $6 trillion (calculations from *Institutional Investor*, 1998) – 25 per cent of all the attributed world financial portfolio assets for 1995.

The combination of complex financial instruments, the potential for rapid changes in risk profile, the enormous concentration of funds in institutions, or financial conglomerates with a range of financial and banking functions, along with the financial integration of institutions within the developed markets, all give rise to an important issue. This issue concerns the cumulative implications, or knock-on effects, of policy mistakes *within and among the financial institutions themselves*.

Hedge funds are interesting in this context because, although they appear relatively small in the panoply of financial institutions, the implications of their activity for that broader panoply can be startling. Some estimates put their total size at $100 billion, others at $400 billion (*Banker*, 1998). The overseas, or non-domestic, investment assets of pension funds alone is many times these figures, with pension-fund and pension-related investment assets of other institutions in emerging markets approaching the lower figure for the total assets of hedge funds. Emerging-market hedge funds amounted to $7.1 billion of assets in 1997, from $0.7 billion in 1992 (World Bank, 1998, p. 17). Pension-fund assets in emerging markets were ten times the 1997 figure for specialist emerging-market hedge funds.

However, when we consider the situation more closely, we can see some aspects of the institutional risk factor described above. The IMF itself observes that the financial institutions have been an important source of funds for emerging markets,

> but they have also led to the growth of highly leveraged hedge funds and proprietary traders [institutions trading with their own capital] who are prepared to tolerate significant risk in their search for weaknesses in foreign exchange arrangements . . . It is estimated that the total assets of hedge funds, proprietary traders, and speculative-type mutual funds have grown to well above $100 billion.
>
> (IMF, 1997, p. 33)

But 'these funds have at times undertaken investments that involved leveraging their capital by between 5 and 10 times' (ibid., p. 33).

The near-collapse of the relatively unknown and inappropriately named Long-Term Capital Management (LTCM) hedge fund in 1998 provides an illustration of the implications, and it opened a new chapter in the global economic crisis. LTCM, the 'Rolls-Royce' of hedge funds (according to the *Financial Times*, 1998d, p. 12), which included two Nobel prize-winners in economics among its founders, built up an investment exposure of around $900 billion (by leveraging to around *250* times its capital base, thereby becoming a very large financial institution by many standards), mostly in developed capital markets, and suffered a 44 per cent fall in net asset value during one month in 1998. Soon it appeared that this could trigger financial problems in other institutions, as bank shares fell on international stock markets. The Dow Jones Industrial Average index of corporate share values in the US fell. The events soon led to a bail-out from other financial institutions fearing a serious knock-on effect within the financial sector. Following the bail-out, some members of the US Congress were preparing to call hearings into how, allegedly, the stability of the entire New York financial system could come to rest on a single, highly risky investment fund.

This added to other problems arising from the emerging markets, as the financial crisis, which had started with Thailand in 1997, spread to Russia in August 1998, leading to a suspension of certain debt-repayments by the Russian government and the massive devaluation of the rouble (17 August 1998 is another important twentieth-century date for Russians, when many thousands lost all their savings in bank crises and subsequent bank closures).

Following the Russian crisis *and* the LTCM crisis, many leading banks had to issue 'profit warnings' (announcements of previously unexpected negative results in forecast earnings) linked to emerging market debt *or* to the superficially insignificant LTCM. It was subsequently reported that many better-known institutions were involved in investing in, or lending to, LTCM. These included:

- the Bank of Italy;
- Sumitomo Bank (one of Japan's largest commercial banks);
- Union Bank of Switzerland (or UBS, Europe's largest bank in terms of financial assets, one of the fifty largest managers of securities outside the US, and owner of Phillips and Drew of the UK, one of the largest UK pension-fund managers), who were proposing to merge with Swiss Bank Corporation to create the world's second-largest bank;
- Credit Suisse First Boston (US/Swiss joint venture, fourth-largest European bank, also with pension-fund management interests);
- Dresdner Bank of Germany (one of the top twenty managers of securities outside the US), and which, along with some other German banks, had ventured into high-risk US hedge funds because of restrictions on expansion in Germany;
- Merrill Lynch (US investment bank, asset manager and recently acquirer of the largest UK pension-fund manager, MAM. Merrill Lynch is ranked as the number-one manager of securities outside the US; it is also estimated to be second only to Fidelity Investments, arguably the largest financial institution in the world, with respect to total assets under management – $625 billion

under management, compared to Merrill Lynch with $446 billion);
* ING (the Netherlands bank, asset manager and acquirer of the collapsed UK Barings Group, which was also involved in pension-fund management; it collapsed allegedly as a result of speculative activity by one of its own employees – a 'rogue trader' based in Singapore).

(*Financial Times*, various, especially 26 September, p. 18, and 2 October, p. 1, 1998; *Banker*, 1998; *Institutional Investor*, 1998; *Guardian*, 1998)

Many institutions took out insurance against default by their borrowers – another derivative, or 'credit derivative' including 'default swaps' – and much of the insurance applied to emerging market investments. But many of those with such insurance subsequently found themselves without adequate cover, or none at all. Part of the problem, apparently, in the esoteric world of financial etymology, has been how to define a default and how to arrange settlements (*Economist*, 1998). This has added another strand to the growing web of interlocking financial relationships of continuing 'derivations'. Such is the knock-on effect of the collapsing pyramid of deals that banks and industrial companies see their share prices considerably reduced and their credit ratings damaged. Profits, growth and jobs are all affected.

We are warned of problems with financial institutions in developing countries (World Bank, 1997a and 1998; and IMF, 1997). There should perhaps be a similar concern for the financial institutions of the developed world. As a result, and in conclusion, alongside the risks of volatility, surges, reversals and contagion, we should also add the cumulative risk of: (a) institutional concentration; (b) the complexity of financial instruments and investment vehicles; (c) the dangers inherent in the technical ability of investment institutions to amass enormous risk at enormous potential cost to institutional savers and banks depositors; and, (d) the lack of 'transparency' of risk profiles in a wide range of financial institutions in 'mature' markets.

Some argue that portfolio investment (including hedge funds and pension funds) are not so important in the financial crises described above when compared to bank finance. Bailey et al. (2000) suggest that bank lending, most of it short-term, was the 'hot money' in the recent financial crises. Most of this short-term lending was inter-bank lending which the domestic banks then lent on for longer-term projects. When the questions of profitability and local economic stability arose, the banks were the first to not renew the loans. Portfolio investors were less prone to withdraw so immediately.

According to this argument, bank finance has become more volatile than portfolio finance because of the pressures on traditional bank lending in the early 1990s arising from the 'fiercely competitive environment' that the banks faced (Bailey et al., 2000, p. 103). This resulted in pressure from shareholders to increase returns by lending to emerging markets. This lending was made on a short-term basis – the classic 'hot money' scenario. This may be true, but one has to ask who the shareholders were of the banks which entered the emerging markets. The shareholders were again pension funds – the short-term investors trying to maximise liquidity. As we shall see in Chapter 8, pension funds (in the UK at least) invested disproportionately in the financial sector in the 1990s, before the investment bubble of technology stocks took off towards the end of the decade.

So it is not so easy to escape the pervasive influence of pension-fund investment. Unfortunately, the conclusions of the comparative study of banks and portfolio investors are perverse.

> To counter a retreat by traumatised emerging economies, policy makers must promote domestic capital market development and *encourage the transition from banks to capital markets* . . . Rather than hiding behind the false security of financial isolation and capital controls, such countries need to equip themselves to become full-fledged participants in the global market.
>
> (ibid., p. 109, my emphasis)

INSTITUTIONAL INVESTMENT AND
ECONOMIC GROWTH

The World Bank, in probably its most elevated rendition of the abstract capital-market theory, suggests that financial integration, whether on the national or international level, severs the link between local savings and local investment and allows savings to gravitate towards the most rewarding projects regardless of location, so enhancing the productivity of global capital, increasing world production and reducing the cost of capital for the most productive economies. Integration is said to encourage an acceleration of investment by augmenting local savings and increasing local growth rates. All this in turn will lead to domestic financial deepening, higher investment and faster productivity growth (World Bank, 1997a, pp. 154–7). As we have noted, the increase in private pension investment flows has been an important part of the general increase in international financial flows. The overall theory however seems somewhat fanciful.

Some have argued that the increase in private pension provision and associated contractual savings arrangements will not have the positive effects on economic growth locally within one country's savings and investment market, or internationally through diversified portfolio management, which the advocates of increasing financial integration suggest (Singh, 1996, Singh and Weisse, 1998). We noted the surges in investment flows to developing countries earlier, along with the substantial reversals which can occur. In their case study of Mexico, Singh and Weisse noted the tendency of the capital inflows to lead to an increase in consumption rather than investment. The deteriorating macroeconomic performance of Mexico and the enormous flows of capital into the country suggest, they argue, that the primary motive of investors was speculative and not based on economic fundamentals (Singh and Weisse, 1998, p. 614).

There is also a psychological effect in liberalisation that creates unrealistic expectations about growth in assets generally. Perhaps most important, Singh and Weisse note that external financial liberalisation leads to an interaction between two inherently unstable markets – the stock market and the foreign exchange market. When there are economic shocks, they argue,

> the relationship between these two unstable markets can lead to a negative feedback loop and even greater instability. This, in turn, would affect other important economic variables such as investment, exports and imports (through exchange rate fluctuations), and consumption (through the wealth effects arising from stock market fluctuations).
>
> (Singh and Weisse, 1998, p. 615)

The ability of stock markets to perform the economic development function depends on both the efficiency of the pricing process and the takeover mechanism (Singh, 1996).

We have already noted the surges and reversals in portfolio flows. Prices in several developing country stock markets increased significantly in the first part of 1997. The stock market in Indonesia, for instance, rose 14 per cent, Brazil 79 per cent, Chile 10 per cent, Russia 129 per cent. But the second half of the year saw major reversals of these figures with Indonesia at minus 45 per cent, Brazil minus 22 per cent, Chile minus 16 per cent, and Russia minus 3 per cent (World Bank, 1998, p. 12). These were accompanied by associated falls in exchange rates, confirming the links between the two volatile markets. The concern noted by Singh is that world share prices – the pricing processes referred to earlier – do not reflect fundamental values and that markets are dominated by 'noise traders' (short-term speculation) and by whims and fads (Singh, 1996, p. 31).

This short-termism is compounded by the failings of the takeover process. Empirical studies suggest that selection in the market for corporate control – a major function of developed stock markets – is not based on rates of return or prices, but rather on size.

> Thus, a large, relatively unprofitable corporation has, other things being equal, a much smaller chance of being taken over than a small, much more profitable firm.
>
> (Singh, 1996, p. 31)

Further, the presence of large and potentially predatory business groups in many developing countries makes it likely that the development of the takeover mechanism in LDC [less-developed countries] markets will increase the aggregate level of concentration in the economy and probably will increase allocative inefficiency.

(Singh and Weisse, 1998, p. 616)

This, incidentally, would add to the economic importance of many allegedly inefficient, if not corrupt, large enterprises in developing countries which are often accused of 'cronyism' and contributing to the excessive bank borrowing and general unrealistic credit expansion which formed a part of the financial crises.

As part of the 'structural reform' process in many developing countries, investment regimes have been deregulated, the role of the public sector in production sectors has been reduced, both of these with a view to introducing greater private investment, including foreign participation. Of the $112 billion of privatisation proceeds received by developing countries during 1988–94, almost 42 per cent was from foreign investors. In 1994, this amounted to 50 per cent (World Bank, 1997a, p. 102).

The relative merits of bank-based versus capital-market-based financial systems and their contributions to economic growth, have been subject to extensive research, particularly in the developed world. There is a high correlation between countries with large private pension funds invested on stock markets, the size of those markets, the level of takeover activity and whether the country can be characterised as capital-market-based. If the pricing process is inefficient, if takeovers do not contribute to aggregate economic efficiency (Singh and Weisse, 1998, and Singh, 1996, summarise some of the extensive empirical evidence), and if the stock markets are unstable or volatile, then there is a very strong case for reconsidering the whole strategy of 'structural reforms' for developing countries, and for private pension fund arrangements too.

ECONOMIC POLICY RESPONSES

There are policy responses open to developing economies to counter some of the negative effects of financial integration (World Bank, 1997a).

These 'challenges to macroeconomic management' arise from concerns over: (a) 'macroeconomic overheating, which results from an excessive expansion of aggregate demand as a consequence of capital inflows'; (b) the 'potential vulnerability to large, abrupt reversals of capital flows because of changes in creditor perceptions'; and, (c) the 'more general, long-term implications of financial integration for the conduct of macroeconomic policy'. Moreover, 'policymakers will need to face these and other shocks with reduced policy autonomy' (World Bank, 1997a, p. 171).

Among other measures, policy-makers can attempt to place controls on gross capital inflows, through capital controls, for example. They can also liberalise capital outflows or accelerate the repayment of public debt in order to reduce net inflows – the overall effect of these measures being to act directly on the financial flows themselves. Other measures are more indirect.

The World Bank felt, in 1997 at least, that even if capital controls are effective, they distort private economic decisions. Other measures include exchange rate policy, trade liberalisation and other influences on the capital and current accounts of the countries affected. An important element is the 'sound' conduct of economic policy, which means prudent or tight fiscal and monetary policy in order to control demand. The impact of many measures has to be deflationary. Following this, the financial crises of the late 1990s have certainly resulted in further massive deflation, impacting on employment and enterprises, whether efficient and profitable, in the traditional sense, or not.

The World Bank itself opines that the monetary and fiscal 'tightening' required to restore confidence 'has undermined growth prospects in several emerging markets'. Furthermore, 'Despite impressive macroeconomic performance and prudent fiscal policies, east Asian economies have become increasingly vulnerable during the 1990s' (World Bank, 1998, p. 29).

Nothing could prevent what the World Bank describes as 'a self-fulfilling loss of market confidence' (World Bank, 1998, p. 30).

> Both healthy and insolvent firms suffered because of the lack of transparency (investors, unable to distinguish among firms, withdrew from all of them [!]), the effect of the currency depreciation on dollar-denominated debt [foreign borrowings accounted in hard currency becoming more expensive to repay], the increases in interest rates to defend the currency, the contraction in credit resulting from the rapid drop in equity of highly leveraged financial institutions (due both to their own losses and to the insolvency of their borrowers), and increased uncertainty and the economic downturn.
>
> (World Bank, 1997a, p. 30)

In conclusion:

> The globalisation of financial markets, driven in part by population ageing and other structural factors, is reflected in the quicker international transmission of short-term price movements in financial markets, as occurred in the Mexican crisis of 1994–95, the ongoing Asian crisis and the recent Russian turmoil and their impact on OECD financial markets. Financial integration has also increased the potential intensity and duration of the attacks. There is evidence that pension funds and other institutional investors have played a crucial role at times in determining asset prices in emerging financial markets, with shifts in institutional investor sentiment occasionally contributing to increased volatility in markets.
>
> (OECD, 1998b, p. 62)

Interestingly, the Chief Economist of the World Bank, whose comments on the World Bank report *Averting the Old Age Crisis* we noted earlier, drew attention to the social consequences of the global economic crisis of 1997–98 and the way in which financial-sector liberalisation can greatly increase the risk of a crisis: 'Almost every country in the world has been affected to some degree.' In just a few months, he added, some countries went from robust growth to deep recession. He points to 'children dropping out of school, millions of people either falling back into poverty or coping with already desperate circumstances, and poorer health' (*Financial Times*, 1998b, p. 20).

The countries affected by the East Asian financial crisis saw 13 million people lose their jobs. Real wages collapsed (40–60 per cent in Indonesia). In Indonesia, 40 million people (20 per cent of the population) fell below the poverty line. In Korea and Thailand, 12 per cent of the population were expected to be similarly affected. It is reported that the number of poor people in East Asia will increase over the two years to 2001 from 40 million to over 100 million. An analysis of 300 economic crises in over eighty countries shows that output growth can recover after one year, but real wage growth takes four years and employment five years (UNDP, 1999a, and UNDP, 1999b).

PROPOSED SOLUTIONS TO FINANCIAL CRISES

The recipes proposed by official bodies vary, sometimes significantly. Whether capital controls are introduced, or greater reserve funds of one sort or another are introduced to counter speculative attacks, or the financial securities infrastructure is developed and better regulated, banking systems and accounting standards strengthened, they all take the pension funding consequences of the ageing population forecasts as given. Indeed, if pension arrangements continue down the road of pre-funded systems invested on stock markets with broad diversification to account for risk, then we are left with the remedies for the dangers of financial integration through stock-market development and international financial flows as they are stated, rather than tackling the root cause of the issue, namely the unrelenting growth and consequences of funded pension arrangements.

It is difficult to envisage a system of greater regulation in developing markets, as proposed by all the official bodies, solving the basic issue – the continuing growth in the funds searching for capital-market investment. Regulatory systems in the developed markets appear to have done little to avoid the extravagant build-up and near-collapse of LTCM with all its implications for the financial structure of the developed financial world.

Both the World Bank and the IMF have conducted research on the history of banking, financial and currency crises. There have been banking crises in sixty-nine countries since the late 1970s. Almost three-quarters of the member countries of the IMF have experienced significant banking-sector problems between 1980 and 1995. There have also been eighty-seven currency crises since 1975. Crises typically provoke recession or enormous fiscal costs and effects on growth. The crises have not been confined to developing countries but have included the US, Scandinavia and Japan.

There is also a connection between the developed world and the developing world in so far as crises have been promoted by excessive funds flowing from the former to the latter, as happened with the Latin American debt crisis and the Asian financial crisis (*Financial Times*, 1998c, p. 22, for overview).

> Moreover, whether retired OECD workers get most of their consumption through (funded or unfunded) public or private pension schemes, their consumption will be derived from the output of future workers and the future capital stock. *The negative implications of slow growth will be the same whether pension incomes come from public or private sources.*
>
> (OECD, 1998c, p. 90, my emphasis)

This relationship between growth and returns has been a recurring theme in our discussions.

8

Arbitrage Capitalism

Pension funds underlie many of the statements, assumptions and conclusions about the growing 'globalisation' of economic life because of their universal presence or potential presence. Following many of the preceding arguments, I now suggest that pension funds are a fundamental part of the speculative, post-Cold War capitalism that has arisen particularly during the 1990s – the new capitalism of 'arbitrage'. 'Spot capitalism' is another, perhaps melodramatic, characterisation which attempts to sum up the events we see happening around us. Maybe also after the 'Cold War' we have the 'Gold War', as portrayed by the arguments concerning the real value of financial returns and the role of stock markets in producing the metaphorical pot of gold for retirement! The role of finance and financial institutions, and the conflict over their role and the control of money rather than ideas, becomes paramount.

In other words, the change in the nature and financing of the welfare state or social security has underpinned or significantly contributed to the new economics of liquidity and financial integration, summed up by the imperative of 'freedom of capital movement' – the exploitation of 'investment' opportunities by enabling finance to come and go at will. This, in my view, characterises the latest stage of economic development in many parts of the world. It has implications for the structure and development of capitalism in different countries which are affected by the new stock-market 'culture' in which pension funds figure so significantly.

We have already considered three things of importance which are relevant here:

- first, we have considered the various arguments and questions arising from the concept of 'rate of return';
- second, we have examined the many questions raised by the role of stock-market activity as an indicator of real economic investment and growth;
- and, third, we have examined the role of pension funds in emerging markets and financial crises.

Since pension funds are now so important in financial markets and investment activity, it is appropriate to consider these funds, and their control, in a broader context of the categories and theories of economic development. What does 'freedom of capital movement' really mean for this post-Cold War phase of capitalism?

We should also remind ourselves that the essential part of the stock-market theory is investment in equities – the stocks and shares of private companies. Markets in securities include government and other public-sector securities too, and these have been extremely important for the development of capital markets (Henwood, 1998).

But equities are paramount in my analysis. Governments which impose a limit on the maximum percentage of equities which can be held by pension funds, or conversely, impose minimum requirements on public stocks which should be held, are dismissed as 'restrictive' by critics and many official bodies. A concentration on investment in public stocks, and therefore the funding of government debt through cheap loans as a result of the mandatory requirements of pension fund investment – which thereby lowers the cost of public borrowing and expenditure – is anathema to the Anglo-American theory, which aims to reduce the role of the state. This is notwithstanding the fact that financial intermediaries have made enormous profits from dealings in government debt, an essential part of paying for the allegedly insidious growth in government expenditure.

The implication of the 'freedom of capital movement' thesis, and its search for equity and equity-related investments, is that the funding of the welfare state is having significant effects, not just on portfolio activity and international speculative financial flows as discussed in the last chapter, but on the whole structure of corporate and general economic development worldwide. It is said to encourage the expansion of production or productive capital, but we can see from the evidence that it does no such thing. More and more funds require rates of return unmatched by real productive growth.

ECONOMIC DEVELOPMENT THEORY

Elmar Altvater has provided a very interesting initial typology and analysis of the different approaches to capitalist development, taking particular care to place these in the era of post-socialist changes (Altvater, 1998). I believe that the development of pension funds, the free movement of capital and stock-exchange capitalism are all increasingly bound up with the 'transition' of many economies, and the further development of others outside the former Communist bloc, following the end of the Cold War.

Even so-called developed economies, as we have seen, are under pressure to 'reform' and introduce stock-exchange-based financial, production and social security systems. 'The free movement of capital' in search of the highest 'return' is a fundamental tenet which provides the rationale for all of this. The new 'arbiter' of growth, welfare and economic decision-making has led to 'arbitrage capitalism'.

This concept of 'arbitrage capitalism' I employ as a term to describe a certain system of profit-taking from dealing in securities as follows: it exploits differentials in market returns within similar asset categories (certain shares in energy companies, for example, may be paying less than others, while their underlying value appears similar). It uses short-term assessments of market movements and advantage, on the assumption that prices may indeed get out of line with underlying values, but only for a short time, during which profits can be made.

Altvater first discusses 'modernisation theory' and the 'transition' process. This is determined by a 'binary logic' in which there are only inefficient systems (in this case socialism) and efficient modern market capitalism. There is no in-between as proposed by 'convergence theory' or its variants, in which there could be a mixed approach between capitalism and socialism.

Next there is 'dependency theory', in which, contrary to modernisation theory, it is impossible for all countries in the world to modernise according to the best practice of market capitalism. What will happen instead is the 'development of underdevelopment' (Altvater, 1998, p. 592).

'Structural heterogeneity' in peripheral economies is also a factor which prevents the development of coherent economic, social and political systems as required by modernisation theory and also, I would add, the prerequisites of the World Bank. Furthermore, 'regulation theory', Altvater continues, reveals a degree of compatibility between economies at different stages of development which drives overall economic growth.

'The regulation of money, moreover, determines the position of a given country in the global currency competition' (ibid., p. 593). He concludes that the process of transition or transformation 'is resulting in a hybrid form of capitalism which is quite different from both the optimistic promises of modernisation theory and from the pessimistic prognosis emanating from dependency theory' (ibid., p. 593).

Following a discussion of extraction-based (primary goods, 'damned to underdevelopment') economies and production-based economies, Altvater suggests that we now have a system of arbitrage capitalism based on the exploitation of differentials in time and space. This, in my view, underlies the structure and dynamic of pension-fund investment activity and its continual search for the highest return as well as the maximum liquidity in order to achieve, supposedly, that highest rate of return. This is where 'money appears to produce more money without any interference of an extraction and production process in which labour is exploited'. 'Therefore', he argues, in a similar vein to the thesis of Arrighi (1994) who also uses the seminal work of Ferdinand Braudel,

> the formula M-M' (money M transforms into more money M') rules the system without the interference of extraction of resources and of the production process of commodities. Arbitrage was a characteristic of pre-industrial merchant capitalism. Profits were made by mere exchange in circulation without time and space intensive production, with economic interests directed to the exploitation of spatial and temporal differentials of commodity chains. Arbitrage therefore is very conservative because it does not stimulate changes of the mode of production nor innovation of its technical basis and social organisation.
>
> (ibid., p. 601)

This is very similar to what we have seen with the unproductive nature of pension fund investment.

Thus, he concludes,

> At the end of the twentieth century, even the most developed capitalist countries have returned to a new form of arbitrage capitalism fostered by financial innovations and the rapid growth of financial markets. It is as exploitative as pre-industrial merchant capitalism but on a larger global scale. In the world of arbitrage capitalism, circulation chains have an hierarchical order. At the apex are the big players of the international financial system who exploit differentials of interest rates, exchange rates and stock market quotations. They are moving huge amounts of capital from one place to the other following the smallest differentials in the global space, and in so doing triggering currency and financial crises affecting even big economies.
>
> (ibid., p. 602)

Peter Drucker (1997) has employed some intriguing imagery by referring to this world money as 'virtual money', but with real power.

It is not being created by economic activity, like investment, production, consumption or trade. It is created primarily by currency trading. It has, or seeks, total mobility (the lack of investment and geographical 'restrictions'), because it serves no economic function and finances nothing. It also does not follow (supposed) economic logic. It is volatile and easily panicked, as indeed we have seen.

THE SPATIAL CONCENTRATION OF CONTROL

The analysis of arbitrage capitalism is extremely useful in our discussions about rates of return, emerging market investment and the general structure of international economic development based on the expansion of pension funds, portfolio investment and the associated logic of alleged stock-market-led growth.

The concept of arbitrage capitalism emphasises the irrelevance in real terms of time and space. Arbitrage activities, the buying and selling of commodities and money, rely on the exploitation of time differentials in space and space differentials in time. But it ignores two significant issues. Surfing the international currency markets is one thing, but, first, the control of the assets is highly concentrated institutionally. The top five fund managers control assets equivalent to the combined GDP of the UK and France, and the top thirty-five control assets equivalent to US GDP – around $8,200 billion for end of 1998. Second, the location in real time and space of the international pension-fund industry is another issue. The enormous institutional concentration is also a geographical one. Arbitrage capitalism is controlled from particular locations – to be blunt, predominantly the UK, the US and Switzerland. In addition, it is controlled from the well-endowed regions within those countries which dominate the control of the worldwide pension-fund economy – 'Wall Street', 'the City of London' and so on (Corbridge, Martin and Thrift, 1994, include many useful contributions in this respect, and earlier, Thrift, Leyshon and Daniels, 1987).

So we have international *arbitrage* – playing with time and space to secure the maximum return – and we have international *control* by financial institutions to secure the maximum income. International *control* is firmly fixed in space, and is indeed heavily concentrated. So, what does this mean for the economies and regions which have such control over arbitrage capitalism? Pension funds and their financial institutions may have their technologies which theoretically make size and location irrelevant, but unfortunately they are still concentrated in size and they are located in particular parts of the world. As Ron Martin has neatly summarised the issue, *space* may be less relevant in the world of rapid information communication, but the significance of *place* remains (Martin, 1994). The financial benefits are enormous for the regions concerned and give us another insight into who benefits from this system of pension fund and financial arbitrage.

On the one hand we have M-M'. We also have, what I will term here, G-G' (G means geography) – there is no equivalent intermediate benefit or spatial effect on production just as money supposedly begets itself under the M-M' formula without the necessity of production. G-G' I think is the spatial equivalent of M-M', according to my interpretation of the ideas of Alvater and the concept of arbitrage capitalism. The arbitragers are located in a particular place, but relative to the money they control, they produce no equivalent benefit for that place or for anywhere else. The benefits accrue mainly for themselves in their particular place because that is where they happen to be located.

We might also describe social security capital as S-S' because, by the same token, the capital is supposed to be self-expanding. The theory that it represents – a net increase in savings and productive investment – is a myth. The bit in the middle of the equation, whether it is M-M', G-G' or S-S', the bit which should represent production, is missing.

Let us consider the UK as a case study. Here we need to describe the UK system in more detail. This gives us a particular insight into the geographical flows of private pension-fund finance (for previous work, see Minns and Martin, 1994, and Martin and Minns, 1995). Why the UK? Given the arguments in this book about the importance of equity markets, the UK contains the world's largest centre for equity investment (*Financial Times*, 2000c, p. 6). By 1999, fund managers in London managed nearly $2,500 billion (1,700 billion GBP) of equity investment. New York was close behind with $2,400 billion, and Tokyo had $2,100 billion. Other centres had much less. The UK is also the leading European member of the Anglo-American bloc, with the smallest pension provision arising from the state. This may, therefore, give some insight into the implications of the further extension of the Anglo-American model for the flows of capital in Europe itself.

I will describe the growth and the investments of the pension funds in the UK, and examine how the management and investment of the funds has become centralised, both in terms of the concentration of control in the hands of a few private financial institutions and more especially in terms of the concentration of management and investment geographically. The point is to examine not just the poor effect on 'capital formation' and 'capital stock', but the geographical, or spatial, implications of this. Who benefits in the world of financial and pensions arbitrage has implications for different regions and countries. In the supposedly globalised world of finance, where does the money and profit really end up?

THE CONCENTRATION OF THE UK SYSTEM

The UK system is enshrined in the 1975 Social Security Pensions Act, which represented an unwritten bi-partisan pact between the (Old) Labour and Conservative parties at the time on the balance of public and private provision of pensions. The Act required that all employees earning more than the National Insurance 'lower earnings limit' should receive two pensions – the basic national insurance retirement pension and a second provided by either the employer or the state.

The second state pension is known as SERPS (the State Earnings-Related Pensions Scheme). Employers can 'contract out' of SERPS and provide a private scheme in its place. These contracted-out arrangements have to provide at least as good a pension as SERPS, but the employers and employees receive a rebate on their state national insurance contributions. Some employer-provided schemes are run alongside SERPS, that is, the schemes are not contracted-out. Contributions to employer-provided arrangements are tax-deductible, and no tax, for the most part, is paid on investment returns. However, pensions in payment are taxable.

The system was disrupted by the 1986 Social Security Act, which attempted to introduce greater individual choice by encouraging further private provision. It made the existing arrangement for employer-provided schemes voluntary, and it sought to encourage money purchase schemes (defined-contribution as opposed to defined-benefit schemes). This was contained in a 'personal pension' system which enabled individuals and employers to contribute to a scheme which would be a personal arrangement between the individual and a pension provider (usually an insurance company). In practice employers contributed very little. These personal pensions were aimed at being more 'portable' between employers without the employee suffering from unfavourable 'transfer values' when changing jobs, or from a 'deferred pension' from a previous employer depreciating over the years as a result of inflation.

The effect of the employer-provided pensions system has been of widespread significance. The system had already grown significantly by the time of the legislation. In terms of membership, just after the Second World War, employer-provided schemes covered 15 per cent of the workforce, but by the late 1960s this had grown to 50 per cent as a result of increasing prosperity and competition for labour. The official figures provided by the Government Actuary (Government Actuary, 1991) show that by 1987 some 10.5 million employees in employment, or 49 per cent of the workforce, were members of employer-provided schemes at that time. There were another 2.6 million people who were not in a scheme by virtue of their current employment but who expected to receive a pension in respect of former employment. These schemes cover both the public and private sectors. Not all are invested, but most are. In the public sector, the public corporation schemes and local government schemes are invested, while others, such as the one for civil servants in central government, are not.

By 1993, in addition to the employer-provided schemes, or 'occupational' schemes as they are known in the UK, over 5 million people had taken up personal pensions: this figure largely comprised those who had left SERPS and, to a lesser extent, occupational schemes, for personal pensions following the 1986 Act. However, by the end of 1993, increasing concern about these pensions was growing into what became known as the pensions mis-selling scandal, because an estimated half million people had been persuaded by insurance companies to change from schemes which offered better benefits. A major but slow review was launched, and insurance companies started to provide for compensation in their accounts. The first compensation awards were made in 1996. Both political parties propose to increase personal pensions of one kind or another (called 'stakeholder' pensions by New Labour, and previously 'Basic Pension Plus' by the Conservatives) as part of the continued shift to private investment as a way of addressing welfare issues.

One of the welfare issues is that the operation of occupational schemes is skewed by company size, sector and socio-economic group. The larger the employer, the greater the proportion of the workforce covered. For instance, in 1991, 38 per cent of men and 40 per cent of women employed in organisations with between three and twenty-five employees were members of employer-provided occupational schemes while the figures for men and women in organisations with 1,000 or more employees were 87 and 80 per cent respectively. The percentage coverage (figures for men only) in the public sector (83 per cent), coal-mining before the restructuring and privatisation of the remaining sector (85 per cent) and banking (65 per cent), contrasts with construction (45 per cent), distribution (38 per cent) and agriculture

(17 per cent). Finally, 75 per cent of full-time professional men and women belong to occupational schemes compared to 44 per cent of unskilled workers.

There have been two main financial implications of these developments. The first relates to the substantial flows of money involved. Between 1984 and 1991, total employer and employee contributions averaged around 9–10 billion GBP per annum, peaking at 10.4 billion in 1989. Over the same period, investment returns (rents, dividends and interest receivable) ranged from 7.7 billion to 16.8 billion GBP (1991). As a result of the increasing 'maturity' of schemes, however, as the ratio of pensioners to contributors increased, by 1987, pension payments had begun to exceed contributions (CSO, 1993). By 1993, most workers were drawing pensions well before official retirement age, with 80 per cent taking some form of early retirement (Incomes Data Services, 1993). In addition, substantial reductions in contributions have been made by employers taking contribution 'holidays' in response to perceived 'surpluses' in their pension funds, as required by the 1986 Finance Act.

Second, these flows have led to a significant pool of accumulated assets. In 1968, the total assets of the pension funds amounted to 8.1 billion GBP, or 50 billion at 1996 prices. By the end of 1996, they had grown to over 600 billion. This is a figure equivalent to over 70 per cent of UK GDP and represents the largest pool of pension fund assets in the European Union. So, whereas the membership of occupational pension schemes had stabilised at around 50 per cent of the workforce by the 1960s, varying over subsequent years by a few percentage points either way, and despite a relative decline in contributions more recently, the accumulated investment assets of pension funds, from employer and employee contributions, along with investment returns, and net of pension payments, had increased twelve times in real terms in twenty-eight years.

How is all this money managed and invested? The contributions of employees throughout the UK are collected by employers, who add their own contributions and administer the money. The employers, and increasingly the employees, sit on boards of trustees, whose job it is to ensure that the funds are administered properly and invested 'prudently'. In order to ensure the professional management of the funds in their 'trust', the trustees appoint a fund manager to invest the money. The fund manager will either be an in-house employee or department, as often happens with some of the largest funds, or most commonly an 'external' investment firm, such as the investment section of a clearing bank, merchant bank or insurance company or an independent investment company. Management fees are charged for this service. Sometimes the trustees will appoint more than one investment manager, perhaps an in-house manager to invest part of the fund and an external manager to look after a particular type of investment. Frequently, two or more managers are appointed in order to compete with each other on the investment returns.

The funds are invested by these managers in a range of investment 'instruments', predominantly equities, government securities and property, with a proportion retained in 'cash', depending on the various rates and returns in the market. These investments are listed or based both in the UK and in other countries, but around 70 per cent are situated in the UK. Returns from these investments then accrue to the fund and either are reinvested or contribute towards pension payments.

In terms of investments, by 1996, around 53 per cent of the assets of UK pension funds consisted of UK equities, 20 per cent overseas equities, 10 per cent in UK and overseas fixed interest, with the remainder in property and cash. UK and overseas equities reached a peak in 1994 and 1995 at 76 per cent.

In order to examine the management and geographical implications of these flows and investments, I have used a number of data sources. First, information on the geographical location of companies and their pension administration was derived from *Pension Funds and their Advisers* (AP Information Services, 1996). This survey lists the value of pension fund assets by region and size of funds, the number of pension funds with capital values of various sizes, analysed by region and size of funds, the number of organisations with pension funds analysed by region, number of employees and activity, as well as information on individual funds. Altogether, it covers nearly 2,000 pension funds with a capital value in 1995–96 of 400 billion GBP, including almost all companies and organisations with over 500 employees and over 10 million GBP in assets, and about 700 smaller ones. The funds which are omitted from these data will in general terms be the small schemes which have contracted out to an insurance company. This source also enables us to calculate the proportion of funds managed by external managers. Second, I have used data from the Stock Exchange lists of share-ownership by institutions and the distribution of companies on the Exchange by market value. The third source of information is that published in the financial press on the market value of the top 100 companies (the FT-SE 100) and on investment management figures.

The data from *Pension Funds and their Advisers* indicate that just over 50 per cent of the funds and 56 per cent of total pension fund accumulated assets are owned by organisations and companies with their headquarters in the south-east of England. This is the most prosperous region of the UK in terms of relative income and GDP. If the amount is grossed up as a proportion of the total 600 billion GBP pension-fund assets estimated for 1996, this means that 336 billion were owned by the pension funds of these south-east-based companies. In other words, companies with activities and employees all over the UK draw in their pension contributions to the south-east for administration purposes. As we saw earlier, it is large companies which have the highest degree of occupational pension scheme membership.

The important point at this stage, in terms of centralisation, is that although only a third of the UK's working population is based in the south-east, the region administers 56 per cent of the UK workforce's pension funds by value. In addition, the largest pension funds are centralised in the south-east, again as a result of the spatial distribution of companies and corporate headquarters administering the collection and payments nationally. Thus 50 per cent by number and nearly

60 per cent by value of the pension funds with assets over 1 billion GBP are administered from the south-east, regardless of the location of the workforce throughout the UK. The five largest funds, with over 65 billion GBP between them, are in the transport, telecommunications, electricity supply and postal services sectors, followed by universities, gas and fuel refining and supply and the largest banks, Barclays and National Westminster. All these companies and organisations have a workforce which is highly dispersed through the UK.

This concentration in the south-east is important, because economic and political power has long been concentrated in London and the surrounding twelve counties – the area defined for some administrative and planning purposes as the 'south-east'. Not only is London the seat of a highly centralised system of national government but the south-east as a whole contains a disproportionate number of the UK's major industrial and commercial companies: for example, 74 per cent of the turnover, or sales, of the 500 largest UK companies are controlled from London (Goddard, 1992). It is the region where governmental economic policies are formulated and administered, and from which key corporate and industrial strategies emanate. It is perhaps not surprising that pension-fund administration is centralised in a similar manner, giving extra weight to the power and control of one region of the UK.

The pension-fund administration does appear to be less concentrated than it was when I previously examined the situation in 1993. There could be various explanations; the latest data include a number of smaller funds which were not included previously, and there have been privatisations or foreign takeovers, by the Americans and French, of regionally based utilities which were once part of very large UK centralised operations. There has also been the switch by half a million people to personal pensions run by insurance companies, which again are highly concentrated in the south-east but do not appear in the figures. By 1995, their exclusion from the calculations would have started to influence the balance of geographical distribution. Also a few specialist administrators have developed business outside London.

However, for pension funds, the most important point in the argument, in terms of what happens to the flows of money, comes next. Here there has been no decrease in concentration of control. In fact, concentration has increased.

I mentioned earlier that trustees will arrange for their funds to be invested by a fund manager. In 1993, I examined the 2,000 funds listed in *Pension Funds and their Advisers* to establish the extent of in-house and external management. This was an attempt to determine to whom the role of investment manager was delegated, regardless of where the employer's headquarters were situated and the funds administered. Some of the largest funds employ in-house managers, and these include the funds of the very large companies and public corporations, such as they now are. They are predominantly managed from London. However, the remaining companies and organisations delegate to external managers and these are overwhelmingly located in London. In 1993, I calculated that no less than 77 per cent of pension fund assets were managed by external managers, of which a small percentage were based in Scotland. This has not changed. Overall, at least 90 per cent of all pension fund assets, regardless of the employer's location and the geographical source of contributions, are *controlled* from the south-east of England. This is a very substantial concentration of control, even given the south-east's economic prominence.

What is more important is that the organisational concentration is even more intense and goes some way to explaining the excessive geographical concentration. The biggest external fund managers are Mercury Asset Management (until 1996 a subsidiary of merchant bank S. G. Warburg and later acquired by Merrill Lynch of the US and renamed Merrill Lynch-MAM), Phillips and Drew Fund Management (Union Bank of Switzerland), Schroder Investment Management (merchant bank Schroders), BZW Barclays Global Investors (Barclays Bank) and Gartmore Pension Fund Managers (in 1996 acquired by National Westminster Bank, which was in turn taken over by the Royal Bank of Scotland in 2000, further adding to the concentration of control).

In addition, remember that Barclays and National Westminster Banks are also included in the top ten pension funds for their own employees. Out of the leading twenty-five fund managers, these top five pension fund managers control over 2,000 individual funds or parts of them, representing 64 per cent of the assets of the total funds managed (end 1995), an increase of 6 per cent from the previous year (*Financial Times*, 1996a).

Altogether, fund management as a whole (pension funds, insurance companies, investment trusts and unit trusts, many managed by the same large group) reached over 2,000 billion GBP by 1995 (equivalent to two and a half times UK GDP). Mercury Asset Management (Merrill Lynch-MAM) was second only to the Prudential Insurance Company with 75 billion GBP, twice the market value of any company listed on the UK Stock Exchange.

Pension funds are the largest block of funds under management by these groups. Davis (1993) noted an increasing concentration of pension-fund management, and that dominant firms tended to stay dominant. From 1984–91, the top twenty asset managers over these years included only twenty-nine firms. Fourteen firms remained in the top twenty in each year throughout, and only two of the eleven new entrants over the years were able to establish themselves in a sustainable manner. Mercury Asset Management, Schroders, and Phillips and Drew have been continuously in the top five since 1984. This is self-reinforcing, because competition for fund-management business is based on comparative performance and not price. The barrier to entry, Davis concludes, is track record not cost structure. This process therefore reinforces the centralisation of management control.

Where then does the money go in terms of geographical location, sector and activity? I mentioned above that 53 per cent, or more, of the total assets of pension funds are held in UK equities. It is this area that I will concentrate on, because it enables us to make assumptions and analyses concerning the concentration of investment patterns. It also involves an enormous amount of money and power, representing the largest single class of investors on the UK Stock Exchange; the latest figures show that pension funds own 27.8 per cent of Stock Exchange equities (1994) with insurance companies owning 21.9 per cent. Along with other financial institutions such as unit trusts and investment trusts, many of which are controlled by the same group of investment managers which are involved in pension fund management, 'financial institutions' of one kind or another owned 60 per cent of the stock-market equities, which in turn were valued at 761 billion GBP in total, a figure equivalent to 120 per cent of UK GDP (CSO, 1995). The 53 per cent invested in UK equities by pension funds translates into 400 billion GBP of shares on the Stock Exchange. As mentioned above, in 1994, pension funds owned nearly 28 per cent of all shares listed on the Exchange. This had declined from a high of 32 per cent in 1992, the difference being mainly accounted for, again, by the increase in insurance companies and other financial institutions (possibly through the increase in personal pensions).

This finance is not invested equally across sectors and companies. The structure of quoted companies, in terms of size in particular, renders this unlikely in relation to the size of funds to be invested. In total, the FT-SE largest 100 companies accounted for no less than two-thirds of the total value of the stock market, which covers nearly 2,000 companies. Those with a market capitalisation of 1 billion GBP or more (157 companies out of 1,909 in total, or 8.2 per cent by number) account for no less than 78 per cent by value (1995). The 227 companies with a market capitalisation of 500 million GBP or more (12.4 per cent by number) account for 84.8 per cent by value (an increase in relative concentration compared to 1993).

Investment policies generally require a limit on the percentage of a fund being invested in the shares of any single company, and, for contracted-out schemes, there is a legal limit on the percentage of any one company's share capital that can be held by a single pension fund. These policies and rules create a bias towards the shares of large companies, as funds reach the maximum percentage in any one company before they hit the maximum percentage of the fund to be invested. Even assuming the matching of pension-fund investment to the weighting of the stock market (which therefore underestimates the bias towards investment in the larger companies caused by strictures on limiting the percentage holding in the shares of any single company), then pension-fund investment in the shares of the larger companies would amount to 468 billion GBP in companies worth 1 billion GBP or more, and over 500 billion GBP in companies of 500 million GBP or more, leaving less than 100 billion GBP for the remaining 87 per cent of companies on the Exchange.

Looking at the top 100 companies, the FT-SE 100, of all categories of investors, pension funds have the heaviest bias towards this group, investing nearly 70 per cent of their equity holdings in the top 100 compared to a market average for other institutions and investors in general of 66 per cent (CSO, 1995). Pension funds own 27.8 per cent of the stock-market equities as a whole (end 1994), but 30 per cent of the top 100 companies.

Let us examine the geographical, or spatial, implications of this by taking the largest companies, the top 100. The shares of this group amounted to a market worth of 714 billion GBP in 1997. The largest company was, at the time, BP (British Petroleum) at 38 billion GBP. The 'smallest' (that is, the hundredth largest company by market capitalisation in the UK) was the Argos Group, involved in retailing. Of the officially listed FT-SE Companies in 1997 (with various changes in the composition of the 100 since the previous year, and certainly since 1993), only seventeen companies had their main office or headquarters outside London and the south-east. Two were Scottish banks and three were local utilities (gas, electricity and water) which have a specific geographical remit outside the south-east. Three years before this, the figure for companies outside the south-east was lower. It increased, probably temporarily, because of demergers (Hanson), mergers (Allied Lyons and Domeq), and some new companies – in fashion retailing and mobile telecommunications – entering the top 100. Subtracting the market value of the seventeen companies (62.88 billion GBP, or 8.8 per cent of the total) from the total for the FT-SE 100 (714 billion GBP) leaves just over 650 billion GBP of market value for the south-east-headquartered companies in 1997, or around 75 per cent of the total market capitalisation of all equities on the Stock Exchange at the beginning of the year. Thus, as a result of company size and location on the one hand and the size of pension funds on the other, it is reasonable to assume that there is a significant bias towards investment in companies headquartered in the south-east, *the same companies from which the bulk of the savings came in the first place.*

In fact, using the proportions of pension-fund investment in equities and the distribution of companies on the Stock Exchange, along with the number and market value of companies in the FT-SE 100, I estimate that at least *two-thirds of all pension-fund equity investment are invested in the shares of the top eighty-three companies based or headquartered in the south-east of England.* This is a fascinating monetary and corporate centralisation of financial flows.

The sectoral distribution of these companies adds further to our understanding of this spatial bias. There are thirty-four financial, utilities, oil, gas and mining companies in the FT-SE 100, but they make up 48 per cent of the total market value of the shares of the FT-SE 100 companies (around 343 billion GBP in February 1997). The financial sector alone amounts to seventeen companies representing 171 billion GBP, or 24 per cent of the FT-SE 100. Although the reasons for investment in particular sectors are complex, there appears to be a connection between company size and size of the sector in terms of market value, and this has biased the market in relative terms to the shares of certain sectors, in particular the financial sector.

The interesting point about the investment in the financial sector is that this includes investment back into the shares of banks and other large fund managers who are undertaking the investment from the south-east in the first place. These include, for instance, Barclays Bank (21 billion GBP of pension funds under management), National Westminster Bank (28 billion GBP after its merger with Gartmore) and Mercury Asset Management (48 billion GBP). (There were some later changes in fund manager ownership. As already noted, MAM was acquired by Merrill Lynch, first renamed Merrill Lynch-Mercury, then just Merrill Lynch Investment Managers. Schroders was split up and the investment bank was acquired by Citigroup. Gartmore was acquired by Nationwide Mutual. All these were from the US. UK pension funds still invest in many US financial institutions with their UK operations based in the south-east.) I am not necessarily suggesting a high degree of corporate and financial self-investment, although there is some evidence of this (see Martin and Minns, 1995, p. 136; this article I draw on here in terms of some of the text and explanations of the general thesis concerning the cycle of pension fund management and investment in the UK). Rather, the argument is that there is a significant bias towards the shares of particular sectors and sizes of company, and thereby – in the UK, at least – a bias towards a particular geographical distribution of investment. This, in turn, has substantial financial advantages for the region in terms of fees and tax subsidy for pension fund activity. The circuit of pension funds is therefore in reality highly skewed spatially and organisationally, being concentrated in and controlled from London and the rest of the south-east region.

Of course, this investment in the shares of large national and international companies based in the south-east need not simply be confined to this part of the UK. These large companies can in theory use new capital for further capital investment, or the expansion of their business in one way or another leading to increased economic activity throughout the UK or in the regions where they operate or produce goods and employ people. In this way, the fact that the money passes through the south-east, in terms of both the infrastructure of fund management and investment, could be said to be merely a reflection of a centralised filtering and administrative process which reduces costs of administration and management through economies of scale, and is a cost-effective way of producing capital for expansion and new investment throughout the UK.

Unfortunately this is not the case. Only a small fraction of share-buying activity is related to 'primary' investment, that is, the issue of new stock by companies through 'rights issues' for new expenditure or new issues by companies coming to the market for the first time. The

major part of all share-market activity is concerned with the buying
and selling of existing shares from other shareholders, the proceeds
of which do not accrue to the companies in which the shares are
held. Hence the stock market functions largely as the 'secondary'
market, which we have already observed. The proportion of share
purchases which are related to rights issues and new issues is in fact
quite small.

Over the period 1982 to 1992 gross new issues as a proportion of
stock-market turnover amounted to no more than 3 per cent in any
one year, and were mostly less than 2 per cent. If we allowed for capital redemptions to be taken into account, and thereby measured *net*
new issues, the figures would be even lower. From 1992 to 1995 inclusive, the net issues were 1.4, 2.9, 2.5 and 1.5 per cent of equity turnover
for each of the four years, an average of just over 2 per cent (Office for
National Statistics, 1997). This implies that 98 per cent of all stock-
market trading activity was the buying and selling of existing securities,
predominantly in the larger companies as described earlier.

In summary, the substantial bulk of UK pension fund flows and
investments are controlled from one particular region – the south-east
of England – and are heavily concentrated in terms of management
and control in relatively few institutions. Most of these funds in turn
are invested back into the shares of companies predominantly based
or headquartered in the south-east, including, disproportionately, the
financial institutions which control the funds. Little of this money is
applied to new capital investment or business expansion or employment creation, anywhere, especially in the other regions from which
the supply of pension fund flows emanate. In other words, the UK private pension fund system has developed a highly centralised and
geographically concentrated structure of financial control and financial power, in which finance is invested through the stock market back
into secondary stocks of the major companies which make up the
pension-fund system itself.

There are, therefore, significant implications in the UK pension
system for investment control and capital formation. It could be

argued that the UK pre-funded, employer-provided pension system provides considerable benefit and business to the financial system, itself based in London and the surrounding areas of the south-east, thereby benefiting one particular sector and a relatively wealthy region, but that it makes little other contribution to the economic development of the UK. It does not contribute to the creation of a real increase in production which itself can help to contribute effectively and in the long term towards the provision of pensions.

The use of capital markets for welfare provision therefore epitomises the concept of arbitrage capitalism. But the importance of 'place' remains. The funds may appear to float around the globe, or float around a particular country, having no real relationship with the productive economy. But the system is not controlled by some global indicators with no specific location, but by structures of management which have a clear geographical concentration and which contribute little to other areas of the 'globe'. The alleged 'globalisation' of pension-fund investment and assets clearly favours some geographical areas above others.

What, therefore, are the implications of pension funds and arbitrage capitalism for the future – and definition – of the welfare state as we know it?

9

The End of the Welfare State?

We have examined the arguments for the Anglo-American model. The main conclusions are that:

- the connection between the nature of financial systems and pension arrangements has been underestimated by analysts of the two subject matters;
- the extension of the Anglo-American pension model is bound up with the extension of capital markets and the free movement of capital for reasons other than the provision of pensions;
- capital markets are no longer reliant on traditional sources of funding but are now bolstered by 'social security capital';
- capital markets do not produce the welfare and improved 'returns' which are presumed to follow from these arrangements, and the free movement of capital has significant implications for economic stability;
- indeed, capital markets produce side-effects which transform the nature of 'investment' into the maximisation of 'liquidity';
- the same capital markets also transform the nature of the 'welfare state' into a 'welfare market', where financial rate of return is paramount and the social issues concerned with redistribution are minimised.

We are left with the question of whether there is or should be a welfare state in many countries, especially as defined by two important welfare or social security theorists, namely Richard Titmuss and Gøsta Esping-Andersen. Both writers, in essence, conceptualise the welfare state as a state-organised system of social guarantees which, in theory and practice, take people out of the economic exchange nexus. The Anglo-American theory, and practice, in my view, drops people firmly back into it. Simplistically put, people in the state system are seen as actually or potentially a burden, those outside it are not. This then has the implications for conclusions concerning finance and production that I have described earlier.

Richard Titmuss, for example, remarks on the 'public burden of welfare', in which welfare is seen as an impediment to growth and economic development, that, in relation to the UK:

> An increase in public retirement pensions is seen (as it was seen inter-nationally during the balance of payments crisis in 1964) as an economic burden. A similar increase in spending power among occupational (pub-licly subsidized private) pensioners is not so seen. Yet both involve additions to consumption demand.
>
> (Titmuss, 1976, p. 125)

Esping-Andersen writes that the welfare state was a different Second World War concept of society (although he adds that it appeared in Sweden in the 1920s); a state-organised, institutionalised system of social guarantees that, unconditionally, assures adequate living stan-dards to all citizens.

Many of these concepts and assumptions about the role of the state as a quasi-guarantor of income standards have disappeared in the dis-course of 'burdens' and irresponsibility. But, whatever the rhetoric, some argue that there are significant difficulties in changing from the old system and its assumptions to something different.

Myles and Pierson write that reform of social security programmes can slow the rate of spending growth, 'but with rare exceptions will not reverse it' (Myles and Pierson, 1998, p. 3). They suggest that '*particular* departures are available only under *particular* conditions inherited from the past' (ibid., p. 3). This is their application of 'path dependency' theory to social security reform. This may be so, but I have argued here that changes or reforms in pension arrangements are linked to much broader changes and pressures coming from the increasing importance of the stock-market theory of welfare *and* changes in corporate/financial relationships. 'Path dependency' theory, as applied by Myles and Pierson, may indeed explain some of the difficulties in transforming one system into another. But we need to take into account the whole changing relationship in many countries between the financial sector and the non-financial corporate sector as a whole. These broader considerations may allow us to see that adding to, or reforming, a state pay-as-you-go system so as to include a privately run funded system is easier than reversing the process. 'Path dependency' is very useful in explaining the difficulties of reform. But it is not a two-way path. Sometimes there is a shift in the social welfare paradigm caused by factors unrelated, or only partly related, to the welfare issue itself. I put this forward as a hypothesis, because the burden of proof rests on a much longer-term empirical analysis.

Nevertheless, the Anglo-American theory is, at face value, extremely infectious. The upshot is usually to encourage private saving, or to try to encourage such saving, by reducing public provision in governmental policies. Or the theory, through the voices of academics and the press, tries to deprecate welfare or social security which does not apparently equate with the rate of economic growth or which does not produce a certain 'rate of return'. This latter case is like arguing for an approach to 'charity' dating back to late-nineteenth-century capitalism, with its beneficence dependent on a fixed rate of interest – 'charity plus 4 per cent'.

Some believe that the weaknesses of markets have been overstated and their strengths underestimated. Whatever the correct balance may be, the argument in this book is that the weaknesses of markets are frequently not even taken into account in the reconstruction of welfare philosophy. Indeed, markets are now to be boosted for reasons which have little to do with improving pensions provision, on the pretext that they somehow will. The emphasis is more on the market becoming the solution and no longer on it being viewed as the problem. On balance, the state is now viewed as the problem, frequently because, quite simply, *it is not the market.*

Goodin and colleagues state that the welfare state should be considered in the context of a capitalist economy – 'In a capitalist market economy, what the market can be made to do the state does not need to do' (Goodin et al., 1999, p. 5) – but this does not explain why there are such differences between capitalist systems in their approaches to the role of the state; these are partly explained by the different emphases given to the role of the stock-market financial system and the role of capital markets. This is now accompanied by different approaches to the nature of economic growth and the role of public expenditure in terms of social redistribution within that.

In the UK, for example, the Commission on Social Justice (1994, the Borrie report, established by the late John Smith when he was leader of the Labour party and sponsored by the Prudential Assurance Company and trade unions among others), carefully crafted an argument which made welfare centrally dependent on economic growth driven by the private sector. Redistribution is concerned with opportunities rather than money, the Commission maintained. The philosophy behind the Borrie Commission's proposals reveals a theoretical basis which informs a substantial part of the debates about the new approach to welfare. I have based the following comments concerning the Commission's report on a previous discussion of the issue (Minns, 1997, pp. 7–8). Although the Commission made interesting comments about the real difference between funding and pay-as-you-go, it nevertheless ended up advocating an extension of funding as part of its proposals because of the apparent public expenditure implications of any alternative (again taking little account of the increased cost of tax relief implied by the massive extension of private provision of one sort or another). Solutions which depend on economic growth are apparently superior.

Of course, in the new economics (post-Bretton Woods and the theory of controlled exchange rates and targeted public expenditure which is used as a tool rather than viewed as a burden) any increase in state pensions is supposed to have no positive effect on economic growth, saving or consumption. This is the post-Keynesian, post-Titmuss era of economics, welfare and the role of the state *par excellence.* An increase in state pensions is always a negative factor, a 'cost', to be discounted, compensated or not contemplated, with no effect on consumer demand, savings or investment.

There are three main approaches to the welfare issue, the contributors to the Borrie Commission suggested.

First there are people who want an 'Investors' Britain'. They 'believe we can combine the ethics of community with the dynamics of a market economy . . . that the extension of economic opportunity is not only the source of economic prosperity but also the basis of social justice' (Commission on Social Justice, 1994, p. 95). They essentially believe in redistributing opportunities rather than just redistributing income. These are the new creative thinkers.

Next come the 'Deregulators'. Their approach '[e]conomically . . . depends upon the unceasing drive for competitiveness through the ever-cheaper production of what we already produce; socially, it relies upon the reduction of public services and public spending' (ibid., p. 95). These are the Tories, the conservatives, the reactionaries, and so on.

Third, however, come the people described as the 'Levellers'. These appear to be the well-intentioned dreamers who have lost touch with reality, or with the new imperative of 'economic growth'.

> The Levellers are concerned with the distribution of wealth to the neglect of its production . . . Their strategy is founded on the idea that we cannot use economic renewal and paid employment as the basis for a socially just future . . . Theirs is a strategy for social justice based primarily on

redistributing wealth and incomes, rather than trying to increase opportunities and compete in world markets.

(ibid., p. 96)

Thus, again, philosophies about welfare, markets and economic
growth have become crucially entwined. The essential element in this
is the encroachment of the philosophy of property rights. This is now
synonymous with improving welfare by giving people a 'stake' in the
economy and social security through increasing self-reliance, along
with individual savings and funded systems. These allegedly provide a
clearer structure of 'ownership' of a personal entitlement and will
therefore promote growth.

The seventeenth-century Levellers in Britain, especially prevalent
during the so-called 'English' Civil War in the 1640s, believed in abolishing social distinctions and the monarchy, promoting an accountable
Parliament and religious tolerance. Unfortunately, the Levellers were
suppressed in favour of the supremacy of property rights and the triumph of the Protestant ethic (now contained in the concept of
'economic opportunity'). To be provocative, the idea of communal
property (perhaps ironically translated into the 1990s concept of 'community') was anathema to this ideology.

There now seems no alternative to a financial- and physical-asset-
based system in which welfare must be measured primarily in
quantifiable terms based on how much people have personally contributed in financial terms to society and therefore 'own' as their
'claim' on society. As we have noted, pensions are now referred to as
new savings 'products', which people buy as consumers or customers
and treat as an 'asset'. An asset for some is a liability or debt for others.

This contradicts the historical conceptualisation of the welfare state
where 'there was no perceived trade-off between social security and
economic growth, between equality and efficiency' (Esping-Andersen,
1996, p. 3). The Borrie Commission was not referring to some philosophy from the seventeenth century when it dismissed the principle of
redistribution of wealth as something attributable to Levellers. It was

referring to the philosophy or outlook of forty or fifty years ago, pioneered in the UK by the post-war Labour government in its development of what came to be known as 'the welfare state'.

In a slightly different context, Bernard Friot has perceptively expressed the difference in approaches in terms of employment rights. In his view,

> Employment rights have nothing to do with profit-making property. An employee does not receive wages as a holder of human capital whose remuneration is subject to the hazards of an increase in market value [of the company], but as a participant in the distribution of resources stemming from collective work.
>
> (Friot, 1997, p. 20)

So, with all the emphasis on private institutions and capital markets, does the extension of the Anglo-American model signal the end of the concept of the welfare state – the end of social protection *from* the market, as opposed to the apparently contradictory conception of social protection *by* it; the end of (re)distribution which is not dependent on the financial market – a market which in turn is now free from government 'interference'? This 'interference' was once considered essential to be the underpinning of the welfare system. It is now regarded as increasing social 'costs', diminishing growth and no longer valid. It is interesting how theory has changed in such a relatively short space of time. Perhaps there is something more fundamental which has prompted the change.

There are three issues to consider: first, how to define the welfare state; second, how to understand the changes in domestic politics which affect the concept of the welfare state; and third, how to approach the considerations of changes in the welfare state in the context of international politics and, no less, the apparent end of the Cold War – a fundamental variable.

DEFINING WELFARE CAPITALISM

Again we have to deal with various meanings and interpretations of the question. The word 'welfare' itself has different meanings – in the US it connotes what in the UK would be understood as social assistance or income support. In other languages the term is meaningless, reflecting different histories and philosophies. In terms of analysis, some writers concentrate on what *the state* provides for welfare or social security (Gordon, 1988). Others suggest that we should adopt a 'mixed-economy' approach, or that concentration on the activity of the state misses the importance of other forms of collective provision.

It is easy to get lost in the plethora of institutions and structures, whether public or private, when we try to classify systems from an empirical or normative perspective. Basically, the classification of welfare states around the pensions issue, and the assessment of what is 'welfare' and what is not, has to rest on the role of the market in savings and financial returns. My argument is that a particular form of capitalism is actually antipathetic to pensions 'welfare' because of its exclusivity and reliance on the most arbitrary mechanism for the promotion of the public good – the stock market. Whenever it cannot deliver, it turns to subsidy and state support – a singular condemnation of the ability of the market to provide social insurance.

The classification then becomes relatively straightforward. The logic of privately funded provision leads to the erosion of provision in general and public provision in particular. It is not a matter of the technical balance between the basic and supplementary, or whether we have a mixed-economy approach, or universal basic entitlements as part of a neutral balance sheet of risk analysis. If the supplementary is funded through capital markets, there is a contradiction between the philosophies. The basic will be eroded, and the private model will become dominant.

I therefore suggest that the pensions debate leads us towards a central hypothesis concerning the supposed 'complementary' and promotional role played by private provision: there is no country where the introduction of privately run, funded pension plans has been accompanied by an increase in state pensions in real and relative terms. They are seen as alternatives. Funded systems lead to the gradual erosion of state or non-funded arrangements, because they construct coalitions of groups which have an interest in the expansion of unproductive capital markets which favour certain parts of society. This creates greater social exclusion, 'dualism' or 'bi-polar' rather than 'two-tier', complementary schemes.[10]

Esping-Andersen's concept of dualism of the state and the market, and dualism of transfers, is helpful. Flat-rate universalism, in which basic universal rates cannot keep up with rising incomes and rising welfare expectations, inadvertently creates 'dualism', as the better-off, in terms of income, supplement modest basic pensions with their own private arrangements. The dualism of transfers – tax subsidies for some and basic pensions for others – leads to the erosion of middle-class support for universalistic public-sector systems from which the middle class obtains limited benefit (Esping-Andersen, 1990). This is the social and political dynamic behind the dualism which feeds the claims of the financial sector that it can provide superior benefits.

In so far as the welfare state signifies inclusiveness, equal access and, most crucially, non-reliance on the market – the phenomenon whose vagaries partly gave rise to the welfare state in the first place – we must conclude that, because of its dualism and anti-collectivism, the Anglo-American model *does* indicate an end to the traditional mechanisms and objectives of the 'welfare state'.

So far as pensions are concerned, while accepting much of what he argues, I disagree with the implications of some of Esping-Andersen's conclusions about the durability of the welfare state in the face of what I have described (Esping-Andersen, 1996, pp. 256–67). It is not a matter of readjusting structures to a 'post-industrial' era of higher unemployment and lower tax regimes. It also does not matter whether basic pensions or social security arrangements remain. Nor does it matter, as Anglo-American reformers propose, that some people should have their market returns topped up by the state or by a universal charge on all participants which is then redistributed. The real point is this. The pension/stock market model shifts a major responsibility for the production of pension and social security benefits on to the market, albeit underwritten by the state through tax subsidies. By so doing, it gives the financial institutions and capital markets even greater influence over economic and social outcomes and accepts their narrow definition of financial return with its enormous negative externalities for economies and societies. In political terms it exacerbates the divide between those who can secure returns from the market and those who must look to 'welfare' or 'benefits' and who are therefore increasingly isolated socially and politically from the mainstream. Let us consider this political point for a moment.

DOMESTIC POLITICS AND WELFARE

The political point is very important. It helps to explain the emphasis on personal savings in the Anglo-American model and the economic 'masquerade', as Larry Whitmore from the United Nations phrased it earlier. The Anglo-American model is based on neo-classical assumptions of 'rational expectations' for a one-dimensional economic and political 'man', and on assumptions of 'rational' behaviour by financial markets.

Personal savings (especially savings which translate into shares and other securities which are traded on the capital markets) will give people a stake in particular kinds of economic activity. Ideally, this will include low inflation with rising stock-market returns. Savers will become anti-taxation, both for themselves and for business, as well as anti-public expenditure, except where such expenditure benefits earnings from stocks or protects savings (Drucker, 1976).

The model gives the middle-income workers who can take part in the system a vested interest in stock markets, a factor which is seen to be missing in continental Europe, where pension schemes are

unfunded. Workers in such European deserts of financial sophisti-
cation and risk-taking may, it is argued by critics of the European
model, view returns to shareholders as a drag on current wages *and*
on future pensions, the exact opposite to the financial and social
structure proposed by the Anglo-American model. By shifting the
balance so that workers have a stake in shareholder returns then
capital/labour relations should change. Indeed, one senior public
adviser from the Bank of England and other institutions concludes
that funding may also 'increase overall economic efficiency and
flexibility by reducing the conflict between labour and capital, since
with funding, workers do not focus on high wages and safe employment' (Davis, 1997, p. 37). Holzmann, writing in an IMF
publication, additionally suggests that a private pension arrangement 'sensitizes workers to financial issues and enterprise
performance, reducing the dichotomy between capital and labour'
(Holzmann, 1997b, p. 1).

In this new world of classless conflict, winning or keeping the
middle-income vote will therefore depend on a political party's policies towards financial assets and stock markets. The new shareholding
democracy of savers and investors has replaced the property-owning
democracy of borrowers and wage-earners. In parallel, companies with
high debt-to-equity ratios (European model) should be replaced by
Anglo-American equity-based companies with greater rights for shareholders (the Anglo-American model).

Likewise, the state as borrower and investor has been replaced by
the state as saver/privatiser through selling its assets and reducing its
borrowing. If it does not conform, the financial markets will punish
from without, now that they have been fuelled with savings.
Voters/savers will punish from within, now that they have their own
stake in 'sound money' and now that there is supposedly no divide
between capital and labour.

This creates an interesting alliance of social groups against the state.
As the prospective Labour Social Security Minister in the UK wrote,
prior to the Labour party assuming governmental office in 1997:

> The only long-term pension settlement is going to be won when the power
> of the saver is such that no political party risks incurring the wrath of this
> growing section of the electorate . . . The savings will be owned by the indi-
> vidual and not by the state. *It is impossible to overestimate the importance of this.*
> (Field, 1996, pp. 39 and 64, my emphasis)

This is a telling summary of the new ideology, the new political economy of finance and welfare. The individual is the rational saver/voter;
and the financial markets, rather than elected governments, are the
new guardians of the individual's interest against the encroachments
of collectivism and mutual debt (both social and financial).

WELFARE AND 'NON-GOVERNMENT'

This brings us, momentarily, on to the issue of the privatisation of
welfare and social concerns through the establishment of 'non-
governmental organisations (NGOs)', 'civil society organisations',
private foundations and other areas of 'civil society' (non-corporate,
not-for-profit, non-government). These have arisen inexorably as part
of the post-state, post-modern organisation of national and international social welfare. They are no longer one-off or exceptional
movements concerned, for example, with the abolition of slavery or
the establishment of the Red Cross, but have become a crucial part of
social organisation or a twentieth-century definition of 'civil society'.

After socialism, for want of a rough benchmark in time, NGOs,
charities and other similar organisations and foundations have
assumed enormous importance in setting agendas for social reform,
progressive or not. Such activities and organisations used to be known
as pressure groups. But now they are called 'civil society' and they
have assumed an international legitimacy, rightly or wrongly, as alternatives, or vital supplements, to governments in their articulation of
conscience and social concerns. Their direct action and their response
to social issues, which cover environmental, child labour, educational,

poverty, disaster relief, health and other humanitarian dimensions, receive major publicity. In some cases they may not be so humanitarian, depending on how one views some organisations, such as the National Rifle Association of the USA, which are recognised as 'NGOs' by the United Nations. The *Economist* estimated that there were 26,000 international NGOs in 1999 compared to 6,000 in 1990 (*Economist*, 1999, pp. 22–4). 'International' means that they were NGOs with representation in more than one country. Naturally there are far more NGOs which are just based nationally. Figures quoted in the *Economist* suggest that there were *two million* NGOs in the US alone, 70 per cent of which were less than thirty years old. More than 100,000 NGOs were reported to have sprung up in Eastern Europe between 1988 and 1995.

They are increasingly seen as a part of a 'third way' or communitarian spirit which transcends or substitutes for political parties, holds corporations to account and challenges international governmental organisations such as the World Bank. Notwithstanding their criticisms and, by some, physical demonstrations in Seattle and Washington DC against the World Bank, IMF and the World Trade Organisation in 1999–2000, they, of course, have their own organisational interests. When considering the role of NGOs in Eastern Europe, Mirjam van Reisen reports from a major research project on these organisations:

> The problems in Eastern Europe are not only of a humanitarian nature. There are complex political, economic and social issues. There is no systematic thinking among the NGOs – and for that matter the EU as a whole, as to how Eastern Europe relates to the rest of Europe . . . However, the reasons given for justifying both the decision to work in Eastern Europe or not to do so were very similar among the NGOs. Rarely, the motivations reflect an acknowledgement of the particular nature of Eastern Europe, as fundamentally distinct compared to regions elsewhere. The justifications were more a reflection of the specific identity of a given NGO.
>
> (van Reisen, 1999, pp. 4–5)

Part of the structure of this new civil society includes foundations – grant-giving charities which support social enterprises. Michael Porter and Mark Kramer state that the amount of money held by US foundations amounted to $330 billion by 1999 (Porter and Kramer, 1999), most of which is invested in the usual way as described in this book. They remark that:

> No other country in the world can claim such substantial and widespread commitment to philanthropy and volunteerism . . . *Foundations can and should lead social progress* . . . Free from political pressures, foundations can explore new solutions to social problems with an independence which government can never have . . . They could spearhead the evolution of philanthropy from private acts of conscience into a professional field.
> (Porter and Kramer, 1999, pp. 121–2, 130, my emphasis)

Whatever the merits of individual organisations, here we have another attack on the role of the state, with undefined and emotive concepts thrown around, such as 'social progress' and 'independence [non-accountability?] which government can never have'. This volunteerist movement of private support for social change contains thousands of organisations with their own financial and political/ideological dependencies from which one can pick and choose. It represents something like an alternative structure of democratic policy choices. The similarities with other concerns about the role of government and economic growth (or 'social progress' in this case) expressed by the World Bank, UK and US politicians and social reformers are interesting. *It is another part of the delegation of social provision to the market – either the capital market or the new 'social market' – by ideologies and pressure groups of both the right and the left.*

> Growing interest in the political and social role of NGOs may reflect the vitality of civil society in the newly democratised societies of Eastern Europe and elsewhere. Yet it also corresponds to the spread of neo-liberal policies, as states shift responsibility for some of their social and welfare functions to private and volunteer groups. It is therefore understandable

why governments and institutions like the World Bank have often shown a liking for the rhetoric of emancipation: NGOs can be instruments of 'good governance'.

(Morris-Suzuki, 2000, p. 69)

The World Bank in fact made a conscious attempt in the latter part of the 1990s to co-opt or include a wide range of NGOs in its consultative processes.

In conclusion, 'non-government' and the market have assumed a dominant role in arguments about welfare and social provision. My arguments about this are also based on the numerous claims and analyses about the social and political implications of the end of socialism and the end of the 1945–1989 era. Let me elaborate.

THE WELFARE STATE AND THE NEW COLD WAR

The Cold War also played on rhetoric, delusions, fears and antagonisms. It justified all sorts of activity and expenditure on the basis of 'national security' (now all sorts of activity and expenditure are justified on the basis of 'not the public sector'). According to one commentator, it is no coincidence that the end of the Cold War is also associated with increasing doubts about, not just the cost, but also the legitimacy of the welfare state, especially in the two countries which played the leading role in the Cold War for 'the West' – the US and the UK (Kapstein, 1998).

In the capitalist West, according to this argument, the welfare state, as we apparently knew it, arose at the end of the Second World War, when the new threat was perceived as the USSR. Having seen the radicalism after the First World War, and the rise of fascism and bolshevism, governments (especially the US and the UK, even including renowned reformers like William Beveridge in the UK) concluded that social insurance was critical for easing domestic tensions, for building a basis for mass mobilisation – for stability and security. These *social* considerations operated alongside *military* preparations for national security.

> The 'beauty' of the Soviet threat was that it fed *both* the capitalist welfare and warfare state . . . The collapse of the USSR may have brought down not one but two great pillars of postwar capitalist state expansion: warfare and welfare.
>
> (Kapstein, 1998, p. 102)

There is some doubt whether the warfare state has really declined in importance (Achcar, 1998). But the definition of 'national security' itself has changed. It still includes state armaments contracts to cope with perceptions of external threats. But, now that social and labour movements are on the defensive, it has reduced the need for the state itself to respond directly to social pressures. Even more than in 1945 and subsequently, this is left to the private sector. Both warfare *and* welfare can make significant profits for private interests now that, in theory at least, there is no opposing social philosophy and no political impediment to the free movement of private financial capital anywhere in the world – with all the attendant consequences for economic and political stability which the withdrawal of the state now implies for many vulnerable social groups.

In 1996, the US accounted for 33.3 per cent of world defence spending, compared to 30.4 per cent in 1985, the peak of Cold War spending. In 1997, US military spending was more than 85 per cent of the average annual military expenditure (at constant values) for the 1948–91 period (Achcar, 1998, p. 98). So US military spending has barely been reduced from its Cold War heights. At the same time, in 1988, US pension assets were $2,085 billion, and by 1998, the estimate was that they would amount to $5,470 billion – now, it appears, an underestimate. Total world pension assets were set to increase from $3,880 billion to $9,808 billion in the period, an increase of over two and a half times in ten years (InterSec Research Corporation, 1994).

It is as if 'many of America's most cherished projects for the world, once stymied by the Soviet bloc, are now advancing' (Kapstein, 1998, pp. 102–3). The Eurasian model, as a result, is being 'reformed' in many of the former Communist countries. Private funds have been established in Latvia, Hungary, Poland, the Czech Republic, Romania and Russia. There are proposals elsewhere in the Central European region, but the pace of change, the extent of localised conflict and debate about the purpose of change, vary considerably, demonstrating the conflict between the models.

In 1997 the trade unions in Slovenia threatened industrial action over the inability of the country's financial infrastructure and economic policies to cope with privatised savings and the preservation of their value. The government in Slovakia was advised both by the World Bank and by the International Labour Office in 1993–94 and subsequently chose to modify the social security system as a whole without privatisation. In Bulgaria the main concern in 1996 was to stabilise the public pensions system while there was a major banking and political crisis leading to street demonstrations, attacks on the Parliament, and the imposition by the IMF of a currency board to limit speculation, inflation and political instability.

These are relatively small countries. In Russia, however, concerns have been raised by the World Bank itself about the capacity of the financial system to handle such an implied level of private savings. In addition, with unrecorded cash deals or a black economy estimated at 150 per cent of official GDP for 1998, and with ubiquitous tax avoidance, inflationary pressures, speculation against the rouble and continuing problems with pyramid schemes and the financial system, by the turn of the century there were still basic economic structures to rectify before the imposition of a privatised savings structure. The centrifugal forces of the eighty-nine republics and regional administrations in Russia also made the prospects for 'reform' quite complex, since public pension policy could depend on a local administration's assumption of autonomy and its actual possession of financial resources (for a recent discussion of regionalism in Russia, see Nunn and Stulberg, 2000, and previously, Treisman, 1996). The 'balkanisation' of

Russia is of some considerable interest in the assessment of its economy and social system.

By 1998, over 270 private funds had been established in Russia, but their value was only $500 million. The main funds, and those that were active, were established by the large oil, gas, energy and banking conglomerates which dominated the Russian economy and politics. However, the World Bank still believed that, eventually, Russia should move to a Chile-type system, involving individual, personalised savings accounts, once there is an appropriate regulatory structure.[11]

In Poland and Hungary there was indeed significant growth in private funded pension arrangements. By the end of 1999, Poland had twenty-one pension funds with 6.4 million members and assets of around $1 billion with an additional $2 billion expected in the following year. In Hungary nearly two million, about half the active workforce, had joined private arrangements. Five funds held 75 per cent of the market, including a Dutch insurance company.

It is my contention that the European model of welfare and pensions, with its Nordic, Germanic, Gallic and Mediterranean variants, and its implications for the organisation of finance and production, appears as the major opponent to the US and the World Bank model in the new Cold War about pensions and social security. In terms of population and GDP, Europe, as defined here (the Euro 13 in Table 2 – the fifteen EU member countries minus the UK, the Netherlands and Ireland, plus Norway), is about the same as the US. The eleven countries which agreed by 1999 to form a European Monetary Union with a single currency had a larger proportion of world trade than the US, and they were in payments surplus, whereas the US was in large deficit. They are characterised by a different approach to capitalist production, investment and collective consumption. This, for the most part, presents an alternative philosophy about the individual and the collective. It raises serious questions about the Anglo-American theory of 'rational expectations', and contains a number of anti-American cultural, political and economic sentiments.[12]

Hence we witness the concerted attacks on social 'costs' and public expenditure from incredulous Anglo-American proponents. Because of the varying pace of change in pensions provision in the former Communist countries, it will be interesting to see whether the European model and philosophy has any effect on the swing to privatisation in those countries of Central Europe being considered for accession to the European Union. Unfortunately, there appeared to be little about welfare provision in accession criteria, and the general bias towards some form of private, funded structure appeared to be taking hold in many countries, as we noticed in Chapter 5.

This is of more than passing interest to Western European countries. One senior World Bank economist, whom I have quoted before, believes (in a surprisingly tendentious argument) that current pension provisions in the dominant EU countries (defined as Germany, France and Italy) 'are not yet sufficiently burdening the economy (and the tax payers) to justify a more drastic reform approach' (Holzmann, 1997a, p. 217). Presumably, this implies that the allegedly 'burdensome' European system of social security actually appears to be viable in economic and, most importantly, democratic terms. It is an ironic transfer of the old Communist adage about revolutionary change which suggested that things have got to (or will) get worse before they get better. Furthermore, this argument suggests that moves towards funded systems in Eastern Europe could 'positively stimulate the discussion of pension reform in the European Union . . . where pension reform is urgently required' (ibid., p. 217).

This would be a neat reversal of the initial inclination of former Communist countries to consider aspects of the European model for their own systems. This, you will recall, was partly stimulated by the aim of joining the European Union. Now we have the suggestion that former Communist countries, such as Poland and Hungary which are well down the road of private provision and of consultations over accession to the EU, could be a vehicle, or stalking horse, for changing the European systems where the situation is not yet ripe enough for internal revolution – in this case, the revolution in pensions. But the 'urgent' requirement is unfortunately not explained, nor are the changes justified, especially if current provision is not so burdensome.

In fact, Holzmann's arguments (more in Holzmann, 1997b) are, at one level, surprisingly self-defeating. When discussing the changes in Chile, he refers to the great advantages of private, funded systems for the economy. After the usual litany of, in my view, unproven successes which are supposed to emerge from 'deeper', and more 'liquid' financial markets, which will allegedly increase 'factor productivity' and, therefore, apparently, economic growth, he concludes that the

> evidence does not establish watertight proof that the establishment of pension funds has been the decisive factor, or even only an important component, for the impressive development of financial markets since the mid-1980s. The empirical evidence is only consistent with the claim. The healthy growth [no definition of 'healthy'] and development of financial markets after 1983 may simply reflect changes in legislation and the learning from experience and mistakes of the late 1970s and early 1980s. Since the counterfactual of the development of financial markets without pension reform cannot be established, and empirical evidence from other countries with similar reforms is not at hand, *it may actually be impossible to prove.*
>
> (Holzmann, 1997b, p. 15, my emphasis)

He has also admitted that

> closer inspection of the Chilean evidence indicates that the saving effect of the reform is not clear, and that the direct effect on private sector saving was *perhaps negative*. The strong rise in domestic saving was generated by strong *public* saving, more than balancing the direct fiscal costs of the reform, and, perhaps, representing an inverse causality through which higher economic growth as a result of improved financial markets (together with macro- and micro-economic reforms) induced higher saving.
>
> (ibid., p. 214, my emphasis)

To return to some earlier arguments about the logic of what I have called the Anglo-American case, along with my discussions of the crucial argument concerning savings, as well as aspects of the rate-of-return arguments, we now have a considered opinion from an unexpected source that economic growth, caused by exogenous factors, comes first. Savings and returns for pension investment come second.

Despite this lack of proof for the pension-fund case, Holzmann's argument continues.

> Nevertheless, for the emerging economies of Central and Eastern Europe, *such a proof may not be necessary* in order to follow a similar approach. What is important is that their financial markets are still underdeveloped, that pension funds *may* importantly accelerate their development *if* the required framework is established, and that developed financial markets *can* contribute to economic growth.
>
> (ibid., p. 16, my emphasis)

No evidence is supplied. 'May', 'can', 'if', 'impossible to prove', 'not . . . watertight proof', 'evidence . . . not at hand', and so on, all raise serious concerns about such inconclusive arguments, along with the very serious implications and conclusions for the process of economic development, based, it appears, on mere supposition.

Holzmann asserts, however, after this presentation of the somewhat unconvincing economics of the case, that 'pension reform must not be left to social policy specialists, but to economists with different backgrounds, ranging from industrial economics, public finance and financial markets' (ibid., p. 34). Financial markets are simply the *sine qua non*.

Based on many of the arguments in this book, let us now move on to possibilities of change which try to use the evidence which *is* available, even from the maligned social policy specialists, to produce a more productive and equitable structure of pensions provision.

10

Proposals for Change

Markets, free or otherwise, are not a product of nature. On the contrary, markets are legally constructed instruments, created by human beings hoping to produce a successful system of social ordering . . . there is no opposition between 'markets' and 'government intervention' . . . And like all instruments, markets should be evaluated by asking whether they promote our social and economic goals.

(Sunstein, 1997, p. 384)

I have tried to argue that technical proposals for 'reform' are one thing. But the need for change in pension arrangements, if there is such a need, is bound up with other arguments concerning markets and economic growth. Economic growth is, in turn, bound up with different economic models, one of which advocates 'flexible' capital and labour markets. This model argues for greater corporate and individual risk-taking through the expansion of stock markets. These markets will help in determining: (a) resource allocation; (b) the nature of savings; (c) the definition of rates of return; and (d) the ingredients for economic growth.

This is, broadly speaking, the Anglo-American/World Bank model.

THE FUNDAMENTAL ISSUE – REFORMING THE CAPITAL-MARKET APPROACH

My argument has been that we must look even further than this to understand the weaknesses in a funded approach, simply because funding involves markets in stocks and shares, and markets in those stocks and shares raise questions about the relationship between finance and industry, the market in corporate control, the narrow definition of shareholder value and the unproductive nature of 'investment' – the fundamental basis, in my view, of the financial markets.

The stock-market model of pensions fails by its own criteria of improving savings, investment, economic growth and thereby addressing the issue of the allegedly increasing burden of public old-age payments. It fails by its own criteria, because it is not really about pensions as such but about capital markets, the free movement of capital and limitations on the role of the state. But not only does it fail by its own criteria, it also fails by the criteria which are produced to justify the extension of capital markets themselves. This, in turn, is because the capital-market model also conceals other interests which it serves. These are the interests of financial institutions, political movements and governments, international governmental institutions, business and labour. The rise of these new theories and models of welfare and finance has not occurred independently of those interests. The philosophy of welfare has indeed changed over the twentieth century, but it has changed, I would maintain, as a result of changes in the constellation of national and international economic and political interests, and not because the welfare philosophy which prevailed in the mid-twentieth century and earlier has been proven unsustainable in practice.

The issue has also become one of international politics, or even international political theory concerning shared definitions of public- and private-sector obligations and property rights. Here the origins of the world's welfare blocs can probably be traced back to earlier philosophies about social contracts and property rights, and theories of the community versus the individual. The philosophies are linked to various interests at the time. Thus, the Anglo-American philosophy did not arise because of the proven superiority of stock markets, but because of the underlying constellation of interests and the opportunities which have arisen for those interests, particularly after the apparent collapse of socialism.

It has been the argument of this book that the structure of pensions and the analysis of the conflicting claims are quite simple. It is not a matter of the state versus the private sector. It is also not a matter of the technical balance between the basic pension or the supplementary. It is not a matter of funding versus non-funding, or contributions based on income as opposed to general taxation. Instead, it is whether financial institutions, their financial markets and their concept of the so-called 'free movement of capital' all play leading roles. In fact, *the considerations of the appropriate pension regime cannot ignore the knock-on effects for relationships between finance and industry, the nature of investment which follows from this, along with broader social and economic implications of the stock-market approach to welfare or social security.* In other words, the balance between the roles of the state and the private sector is crucial, and the *nature* of the private-sector involvement is fundamental in determining the interests and beneficiaries in the process.

I have tried to demonstrate that the arguments for the financial-market structure of welfare provision are unconvincing. I therefore suggest that we should construct a set of goals for pension systems which contain a different philosophy. These goals will subsequently leave the balance between the basic and supplementary to local factors, but they will preclude an emphasis on privately funded arrangements, particularly those employing private financial institutions and 'free' capital markets. I believe it is essential to be clear about this and not to fudge the issue.

Financial markets as they currently operate do not produce what they are said to produce by the prevailing views of pension-fund investment policy. Recall the discussion about savings and investment or capital formation. As some proponents of the Anglo-American model conclude, if these arguments fall, then so does the whole case. Some commentators nevertheless suggest that high rates of return have been produced. I have suggested that the rate of return is far more complex and demands more radical thinking. Proposals for change should therefore also try to redirect existing privately funded systems which have huge investments in stock markets towards a more equitable and productive result.

I have tried to summarise the Anglo-American theory, its critique and some alternatives as mentioned implicitly or explicitly in this book in Table 7. The table suggests that there is an alternative route to economic growth, if that is the objective. It also proposes a scheme for improving pensions which takes the distributional issue head-on. It does not try to cover up the issue with arguments drawing on

Table 7   Anglo-American Theory, Critique and Alternatives

Anglo-American theory	*Critique*
State expenditure too high, causing negative effects on the economy	A normative not an economic question; anyway ignores positive effect of public expenditure
Ageing populations make the situation worse through worsening dependency ratios	Ambiguous issue which takes narrow definition of dependency; also ignores positive effects of pensioners' spending and saving
Need to encourage more people to look after themselves	Depends on ability to pay
Do this by increasing personal savings, thereby adding to funds for investment	No convincing evidence that leads to increase in national net savings
This will lead to increased investment on stock markets	Does not lead to increased productive investment
This in turn increases economic growth, improves financial returns, personal returns and pensions	No correlation between economic growth and financial returns

Turning the theory on its head

Policy (a) *(objective to increase economic growth)*	*Policy (b)* *(objective solely to increase pensions)*
Increase pensions to increase savings	Up-rate state pensions in line with annual earnings' increases twice yearly, to promote social and political inclusiveness and end poverty in old age
Remove tax concessions from pension funds and transfer to corporate retained earnings	
Introduce tax concessions for corporate book reserve supplementary pensions	State pension minimum of 80 per cent of average wage
	Universal entitlement regardless of need
National Provident Fund to invest personal savings in partnership with industry's plans to invest retained earnings	Tax incentives only for supplementary arrangements based on private or public pay-as-you-go, corporate book reserve, or National Provident Fund models
Tax incentives for pension-fund investment in approved, targeted asset categories	Cap on all fees charged on personal pensions or equivalent of over 2 per cent
Investment restrictions on certain asset categories, especially overseas investment, plus rising scale of tax profits from selling shares within 12, 6 and 3 months of purchase	Tax relief on pension payments resulting from investment in approved, targeted asset categories

the so-called imperative of economic growth through capital markets as the *sine qua non* of more equitable social redistribution.

BASIC AND SUPPLEMENTARY

A high basic and universal pension entitlement is necessary for inclusiveness and to prevent dualism, especially in the capitalist societies which have pluralist systems of democracy in which the middle classes, or middle-income-earners, can be separated out from the welfare consensus. Conversely, the response to those who complain that many pensioners do not 'need' such a high level of pensions provision is twofold.

First, such an improvement would automatically solve the problem of poverty in old age. This problem is caused, in particular in a country like the UK with a residual means-tested system, by pensioners refusing to claim such means-tested benefits. An automatic improvement in the basic pension would go a long way towards solving this. In addition, in other countries like the US, as well as the UK, a change in inflation-proofing by linking increases to the higher of wage increases or prices, instead of the lower, would have the same or an additional effect of the same kind.

Second, those who do not 'need' such an improvement will surely save a large part of it, thereby adding to aggregate private saving which the Anglo-American privatisation lobby desires. To the extent that this policy might entail increases in mandatory taxation, or public saving, then the subsequent switch to saving by pensioners would be a subtle way of introducing a compulsory *private saving* scheme, for which there is such a great concern from some economists.

Third, where a 'supplementary' is deemed appropriate for different local political and economic reasons, there are strong alternatives to the Anglo-American model of supplementary pensions. These include:

- *private* pay-as-you-go arrangements, such as those run by 'social partners' in France;
- private 'book reserve' schemes in Germany, Austria and Luxembourg;
- state-run funded schemes, or provident funds, in the Asian-Pacific model.

The mixture will vary but the objective is, again:

- a high level of 'basic' entitlement;
- a supplementary which is not substitutional or aimed at replacing the basic.

The proposals in Table 7 suggest that fiscal measures can be used to determine the nature of the supplementary arrangement.

DEALING WITH EXISTING FUNDED SYSTEMS

Doug Henwood argues that the discussion of so-called 'progressive use of pension funds' has no part in addressing the fundamental changes which financial systems require: 'The whole idea of creating huge pools of financial capital should be the focus of attack, not the uses to which these pools are put' (Henwood, 1998, p. 306). Indeed. The arguments which I have put forward endorse this. The problem, however, is that huge pools of capital have indeed been created and I am reluctant to leave the subject without proposing that something be done to ameliorate their effects. This may, unfortunately, upset some American critics who suggest that the power structures surrounding pension funds and the investment market generally make it impossible for pension funds to be influenced or, in turn, to have any influence:

> big figures are thrown around to show the potential power of pension funds, should they ever come under democratic control . . . [But] stocks have not been a source of investment funds for decades . . . Since the early 1980s, more stock has 'disappeared' than been issued. The reason is that stocks have become one of capital's more recent competitive weapons in the war for market share, the merger and acquisition boom of the 1980s and 1990s . . . This is a game pension funds cannot play.
>
> (Moody, 1997, p. 68)

Sadly for such commentators, however, they do. As we have indeed seen earlier, the issue is about votes and corporate control, not investment, which has become a dead duck. Pension funds, their managers and pension-related activities have a clear and significant role in acquisitions, as well as in hedge funds, along with emerging-market investment and other activities. All of these issues raise serious questions about the role of pension funds, as well as about the role of the stock market in the production of real investment. As we have seen, the funds and markets play little part in the funding of corporate or more general economic growth and are more important in terms of markets for corporate control.

Interestingly, however, the left in the Anglo-American heartland, or some parts of the left in the birthplace of the capital-market model, see attempts to influence the pension funds which sprang from trade union and labour deals as futile. So much for labour power, one might observe. Conversely, the World Bank and the US Congress see such attempts as undermining 'perfect' (whatever that means) markets and 'efficient' asset allocation. Or, if the state itself is managing the stock-market investments, then this is alleged to be 'a backdoor to nationalisation'. (I refer to the infamous World Bank phrase from the 1994 publication, quoted earlier, and Feldstein, 1997a, also quoted earlier, along with the alarmist responses to the Clinton proposals to 'privatise' social security in 1999, referred to in the section on the reformist movement in Chapter 5.) New Labour supporters in the UK, arguing that increasing 'globalisation' has limited the room for manœuvre by an individual nation, may be shocked at such presumptions of influence on their, or the state's, behalf!

Some countries which have adopted the Anglo-American model have already introduced alternative investment policies, often through trade unions, as in Australia and in the Anglo-American homeland – the US itself.[13] The US and the UK have witnessed the development of socially responsible investment organisations, ethical investment funds, social investment 'screening', along with international link-ups and information flows between organisations about the activities of companies registered in one country but operating in many others. The leading proponents of these activities are local state and local government authorities, some even with significant trade union involvement.

But it is one thing to pass off the need for radical change, in terms of particular countries and companies, by redefining key areas of investment as high-risk or subject to court cases, boycotts, environmental enquiries, economic sanctions and consumer withdrawal, and therefore problematic in terms of narrow financial rates of return, but this is no longer sufficient if the broader picture of rates of return and the implications for the financial system and productive investment are to be taken into account.

Many of the countries in the European model which have small, privately funded systems place restrictions on investment in certain asset categories, especially foreign investment (for example, France 5 per cent, Germany 6 per cent in non-EU equities, Sweden 5–10 per cent), although some of these 'restrictions' are quite loose; Germany also requires foreign fund managers to have a link with a local German manager (IMF, 1997). Sweden has a 10 per cent capital gains tax on pension funds. Denmark allows tax deductions on contributions only if investment returns are taxed – effectively a restriction on investment outside Denmark – and a 50 per cent tax on real interest earned of more than 3.5 per cent per annum. Like Australia, Denmark includes a significant role for trade unions – again, not what the advocates of the deregulated, decentralised, 'competitive', so-called laissez-faire private model, without any external 'interference', propose. Further research over the long term would be interesting in order to examine real returns in many of these alternative arrangements, especially when there is still much argument about the definition of 'rate of return' and pension responsibilities.

Another approach to the investment issue has been proposed by a number of people including politicians, and some of these ideas are referred to by Robin Blackburn (2000, p. 27). This would be for governments to issue long-term bonds dedicated to specific social and infrastructure policies, such as investment in education, health or public transport. The bonds would be restricted to pension funds. This could be administered alongside the pension-fund development index which I have proposed in this book. As a result, corporate investment by pension funds would also take into account the long-term investment by companies in social or economic development.

Since there was so much concern about the international flows of finance on the world's stock markets in the second half of the 1990s, it would be useful if policy-makers in the Anglo-American bloc, which supplies so much capital to these markets, considered investment

policies which were more restrictive, even creative in relation to the
funded systems in their own countries.

I use the word 'restrictive' with some reservation, because it is
used by the Anglo-American proponents to imply some reduction
of 'liberty'. As I have tried to argue, the concept of liberty for financial markets equates 'rate of return' with the maximisation of
liberty for certain individuals. 'Restrictions' on financial markets
therefore allegedly 'restrict' individual freedom. But this draws on
longstanding philosophical arguments about utility and social welfare. The main point here is to argue for the creation of a structure
which does not accept the concept of the maximisation of liberty
and welfare as the one defined by capital markets, which appear to
have taken on the role of social philosophers as well as profit-
takers.

So, where there are privately funded arrangements, we should
encourage alternative structures of:

* accountability – employee involvement and control to encourage
  inclusiveness and ownership;
* management – only local managers, not foreign companies; plus
  controls on fees;
* investment policy – the most crucial area of all; this will include
  incentives for targeted, productive investment, and limitations –
  restrictions – on certain asset categories;
* existing investments – the application of a Human Development
  Index for pension funds, such as that outlined below and suggested in the Appendix.

For the funded systems in Europe, *especially* the UK, they should also
be seen as part of national and European industrial, regional, fiscal
and monetary policies (Minns and Tomaney, 1995).

THE HUMAN DEVELOPMENT INDEX FOR PENSION FUNDS

The concept of the Human Development Index (HDI) pioneered by the United Nations Development Project (UNDP) would be additionally instructive in the assessment of pension-fund investment policies (UNDP, 1999a). Let me explain.

The theoretical and, probably, political issue is that Economically Targeted Investments (ETIs), described earlier, operate outside the logic of stock-market investment and its assessment of returns. They thereby present an important challenge to the entire structure of the Anglo-American stock-market ideology and its definition of 'return'. Indeed, ETIs try to demonstrate that the calculus of narrow financial return is insufficient and may be counter-productive in the assessment of how to create economic growth, employment and income security. They represent a greater qualitative assessment of economic 'efficiency' and 'returns'.

The HDI, mentioned above, even tries to quantify a broader calculus by including measurements of educational and other factors. The HDI as used by UNDP would need substantial modification for the purposes described here. But it would contrast significantly with the delegation of decision-making to supposedly 'objective', quantitative instructions or narrow indices from 'the markets'.

I have tried to suggest some ideas for a 'Human Development Index for Pension Funds' in an Appendix, although it is far less ambitious than the UN HDI and is probably inappropriately named. I have resisted including the word 'social' in the name, since this appears to be viewed in the prevailing ideology of markets as the opposite to 'economic', and therefore unrelated to the creation of real 'value', and thereby a 'cost'. Maybe the word 'human' will be the next to go.

The HDI for pension funds might be used alongside the actuarial assessment and comparison of occupational funds produced by Bryn Davies and Union Pension Services in their 'Pension Profiles' (UPS,

1993, 1996, 2000). Over 200 UK pension plans were assessed in this work against a benchmark in terms of the benefits they offered in return for a certain rate of contributions, eligibility requirements and other indices unrelated to rate of financial return. The HDI investment index would then tell contributors what they are getting in terms of broader economic or social return from their pension plan. Put together, these two indices could provide a reasonable picture of fairness in contributions and benefits on the one hand, and fairness in terms of social returns on the other. (The final variable – what financial return is received on investments – can easily be discovered by anyone turning to the back pages of the *Financial Times*, or national equivalent.)

The narrow measures of financial returns absolve institutional investors of responsibility for calculating the ingredients for economic development for themselves when, in fact, their decisions are crucial for local interest rates, exchange rates and, by the same token, the price of capital. There is, basically, an ideological divide in which participants in the debate about pension-fund investment and its implications for economic growth just talk past each other. It is 'ideological' because there is a fundamental disagreement about basic assumptions. An HDI for pension funds which contained indices of how, even crudely, a company benefits society as opposed to its shareholders, using measures of investment, taxation and dividends, would probably not solve this, but it would provide an instrument for constructing an alternative league table of 'returns'.

These would all be small contributions to shifting the balance of argument about returns and markets. But the other part of the argument has to be even more visible – the protection and expansion of the public pension system. Playing around with investment rules and regulations is no excuse for furthering the privately run and invested pension arrangements, which has happened in many of the countries which have such funded pension structures.

SUMMARISING THE POLICIES

Following on from this, the policy options (a) and (b) in Table 7 should be taken together, because they overlap and are mutually reinforcing. They are meant to be a guide for those countries contemplating alternatives and those already subject to privately managed funding. They draw on all the discussions I have elaborated.

The proposals will:

- increase pensions;
- promote inclusiveness;
- make companies less dependent on the stock market;
- give companies a greater ability to use their own corporate earnings or book reserves;
- increase the demand for government securities by depressing demand for equities;
- lower interest rates;
- control prices of private pension 'products';
- increase productive investment and employment;
- control the increase in unproductive national and international flows.

The aim is to alter the relationship between finance and industry on the one hand, and finance and welfare on the other – the link all the time being the role and nature of the financial system to both production and welfare.

Here I want to finish my policy statement by borrowing a concluding argument from the completely different approach and assumptions of Martin Feldstein in *Foreign Affairs* (1997a). He was arguing for more privatisation as a way of promoting the central, unproven equation and rhetoric of pensions, savings, capital formation and economic growth. I argue the opposite. Thus, in my view of the policy I have just outlined, it is difficult to think of (to quote) 'any other policy' (no less), that could produce 'such a substantial permanent rise in the standard of living of the vast majority of the population' (Feldstein, 1997a, p. 38).

THE BOTTOM LINE

I have certainly been concerned to summarise arguments for and against private funding and to examine some of the extensive literature on many of the issues. But most important is this. Bearing in mind the way in which the private model of funding is related to a complete model of capitalist finance and production relationships, we must consider the enormous negative costs for economies that fund for pensions provision through the use of open stock markets.

In sum (i) the Anglo-American stock-market model, and its variants, as proposed by the World Bank and others,

- is based on supposition and a theory for which there is inadequate supporting evidence;
- supposedly produces 'returns' which, in fact, bear little relation to real productive activity;
- actually generates social returns which are far lower than financial returns;
- and, in addition, produces enormous negative side-effects, or externalities, through its quest for liquidity – within markets through takeovers and lack of long-term commitment to individual companies, and between markets through adding to the flows of uncommitted flight capital;
- plus, finally, it promotes the power and influence of financial institutions and markets over that of governments.

(ii) The dispute between the welfare blocs and their theoretical and normative claims is not about economic growth or capital accumulation *per se*. It is about *shares* in that growth – growth which is caused by other factors. The conflict is about who should benefit from the distribution of existing and future wealth. Arguments about economic growth obscure the basic conflict. In other words,

- The Anglo-American model has constructed an elaborate theory which essentially distributes more income to the financial sector and to the most secure individuals in terms of employment. It rejects the state as initiator, often seeks to minimise state pensions provision, but requires the state to pay for limited social distribution along with substantial financial support through subsidies for the private investment infrastructure.

- The European model, whether tax- or contribution-financed, contains higher universal distribution from the state to pensioners. Where there are supplementary systems, they do not depend on distributing income to the financial sector and they do not undermine the basic pension. There is less acceptance of the issue as economic rather than social.

- The Asian-Pacific model contains a greater role for the state in investment, both for production and general welfare. It uses stock markets but does not depend on them. It does not distribute to the financial sector, does not depend on a 'developed' financial sector and may be appropriate for developing economies and former Communist countries.

(iii) There are clear alternatives to the Anglo-American model. There are also ways of changing the structures and priorities within the Anglo-American model itself. These will actually produce growth, if that is the target, which, so far as I can see, the Anglo-American model does not. They will also produce a high level of equitable pensions, which the unfettered market-determined mechanisms of the Anglo-American solution appears unable to do.

Appendix
A 'Human Development Index' for Pension Funds

How to calculate the Human Development Return for Pension Investments

The UNDP Human Development Index (HDI) is based on three components – indicators of longevity, education and income per head. The 'Human Development Return' (HDR), developed here, is based on calculations aiming to see how much a company pays itself and its investors (salaries and dividends) as opposed to, first, how much it pays to 'the community' (defined as tax paid minus fiscal concessions received, plus additional expenditure on 'social' measures) and, second, how much is committed to future production.

As with the HDI, the HDR is very crude, perhaps even more so, because in my view the quantification of economic and social development is extremely subjective. In market terms, those who believe in the objectivity of stock markets have the advantage in having simpler indicators to consider – the stock-market price of the shares, or the returns from dividends and capital gains, and that is all.

The HDR for pension funds would work, in principle, as follows.

Each company in which a pension fund or pension investor held an investment would be assessed according to criteria or ratios, such as the following:

1. Research and development expenditure (or planned capital investment)
    divided by
    Tax concessions on returns to investors

2.   Research and development expenditure
     divided by
     Dividends paid to investors

3.   Tax paid by the company
     divided by
     Tax foregone on its pension contributions

4.   Expenditure on health and safety, environmental protection
     divided by
     Expenditure on hostile acquisitions

5.   Average payment to employees
     divided by
     Average payment to board members

The results of the calculations are added together to give the human development 'rate of return'. The higher the figure, the higher the HDR for the investor. This would be measured against the average for the industry or sector.

If the equations are inverted and the calculations redone and added together, the investor will get the 'price' being paid. By implication, the higher the 'price', the higher the 'social cost'.

In contrast, market measures are used to indicate the opposite – the higher the market price, the higher the 'value' of the company to the economy and society. It would be interesting to compare the two measures for, say, the top 100 companies by market capitalisation (total market value of their shares) in the US and the UK.

These are only initial ideas for further elaboration and discussion. I am also sure that the analogies with the language of 'the market' could be extended.

(*With acknowledgements to UNDP, which has no responsibility whatsoever for this particular exploration of alternatives to measures which are otherwise concerned solely with calculating 'economic opulence'.*)

Notes

This work has benefited from discussion among members of the European Network for Research on Supplementary Pensions (ENRSP). Since 1994, ENRSP has held conferences and seminars on the operation of pensions in Europe and elsewhere. A series of meetings in Paris, Münster, Dublin, Rome and Amsterdam has brought together researchers and independent practitioners from many countries. This has led to many publications, including books, articles and proposals for a Working Paper series.

ENRSP itself has already produced publications which directly or indirectly examine the assumptions behind the World Bank arguments and which, in my view, demonstrate the weaknesses in the Bank's assertions. Some pre-date the publication of the World Bank report. Others contain contributions to long-standing debates and issues about pensions, labour markets, savings and state policies in different countries.

Previous reports and publications by ENRSP include the following:

(i) Emmanuel Reynaud, Lucy apRoberts, Bryn Davies, Gerard Hughes, eds, *International Perspectives on Supplementary Pensions: Actors and Issues*, Quorum Books, 1996 (ENRSP I). Papers from a conference in Paris, January, 1994.

(ii) Gerard Hughes and Jim Stewart, eds, *Pensions in the European Union; Adapting to Economic and Social Change*, Kluwer Academic

Publishers, 2000, papers from a conference organised by the Gesellschaft für Versicherungswissenschaft und Gestaltung e V and the ENSRP, June 1996, Münster (ENRSP II); the main papers from this are also available in *Les Retraites dans l'Union Européenne: Adaptation aux évolutions sociales*, L'Harmattan, Paris, 1998.

(iii) Papers presented at the Conference of the ENRSP, Dublin, September, 1997 (ENRSP III), some published by Kluwer Academic Publishers in 1999 in Gerard Hughes and Jim Stewart, eds, *The Role of the State in Pension Provision; Employer, Regulator, Provider*.

(iv) Papers presented at the Conference of the ENRSP, Rome, December 1998 (ENRSP IV).

(v) Papers presented to a conference in Amsterdam in October 1999 (ENRSP V).

The abbreviations 'ENRSP I, II, III, IV or V' are used to refer to these various papers and publications in these notes and bibliography, where such references apply.

NOTES TO THE TEXT

1. The World Bank's own pension plan is an occupational, defined-benefit arrangement with high replacement ratios (pension as proportion of eligible salary) (World Bank, 1995). Caufield, 1997, relates how the high, tax-free salaries (with a special allowance for US citizens who would otherwise be required to pay tax), as well as an amazing array of free overseas housing and utilities provision, 'assignment allowances', 'hardship allowances', 'cost of living adjustment allowances' and travel, removal, leaving and joining grants, create a disincentive to labour mobility. The World Bank is also, of course, a public-sector body. Nevertheless, in 1995, this *public-sector* body, with its heavy cost of labour and pension 'liabilities', made a profit of '$1.35 billion for itself, and $6.84 billion for

its bondholders' (Henwood, 1998, p. 50). The bondholders included pension funds. I hope you can spot the many ironies.

2. I use here the three criteria proposed by Weiss (1997) to assess the contentious theme of globalisation: namely, *novelty* (without parallel, not just an 'oscillation'), *magnitude* (comparative size) and *distribution* (how geographically extensive).

3. The European Network for Research on Supplementary Pensions (ENRSP) has already produced a number of papers (see above). In addition, a riposte to the privatisation theory has been given by Leone (1997) and significantly by Singh (1996) and Singh and Weisse (1998).

4. In 1998, the Financial Services Authority estimated that the cost could rise to 11 billion GBP and that half of the 5 million personal pensions sold between April 1988 and June 1994 may have been mis-sold.

5. 'Promotional costs are estimated to account for as much as 30 per cent of operating costs for Chile's AFPs [Administradoras de Fondas de Pensiones].' The World Bank suggests that this may be partly due to decentralised versus centralised management, the former allegedly producing higher rates of financial return. An alternative interpretation is that the relatively high returns in Chile (if they are such in real terms) have resulted from high interest rates, since the bulk of the funds have been invested in government bonds and bank paper (Leone, 1997), as required by law. This has got nothing whatsoever to do with 'decentralised management' as the World Bank proposes. Also see the World Bank's own research: Vittas and Iglesias, 1992. This showed high returns for the period 1981–90, with holdings of, what I understand to be, 100 per cent of government securities, 38 per cent of bank securities and only 9 per cent of equities.

6. HMSO, 1997; G. Esping-Andersen, 'The Double Problem of Co-ordination in Contemporary Welfare States', paper presented to the Conference on Social Policy and Economic Performance, Amsterdam, 23–25 January 1997, the original of which I have not

seen. These reports are discussed in the context of the situation in Ireland by the Council for Social Welfare, 1997.

7. The most recent and comprehensive review and analysis of the savings and investment arguments, some of which are discussed here, is contained in Pollin, 1997. On the role of different types of saving see Robert Blecker's chapter, 'Policy Implications of the Saving–Investment Correlation', and on the role of profitability see the 'Commentary' by Steven Marglin. On the debate in general, see Pollin's own Introduction. The savings and investment relationship is discussed in the context of the 1997 Asian financial crisis in Wade and Veneroso, 1998.

8. The calculations assume that about 75 per cent is managed by private financial institutions and that management fees range from 0.1 to 0.5 per cent or more, depending on the investment 'product'. Add to these fees the charges on personal pension plans (at much higher rates on 401[k] plans in the US mutual funds – average 1.2 per cent expense ratios ranging up to 17 per cent in some cases, with 3 to 5 per cent sales charges in around 60 per cent of funds, up to 30 per cent administration charges and fees in the UK, and 15 per cent in Chile, with promotional costs much higher again), and we have an enormous 'industry'.

9. Bernard Friot argues that the French, privately run, pay-as-you-go system is completely different. 'Retirement income is not a "deferred wage" that a worker did not take while employed and which is recouped later. On the contrary, pensions are the ex-workers' participation in the wages assigned to currently employed workers.' Friot, ENRSP III, p. 13. Also Friot, ENRSP IV, and Friot, 1998b.

10. The latter terminology is drawn respectively from Esping-Andersen, 1990, and Friot, ENRSP III.

11. For Central and Eastern Europe, World Bank, 1994; plus, 'Pensions crisis spurs reforms in E Europe', *Financial Times*, 19 August 1997; 'Pensions boost for financial markets', *Financial Times*, 21 August 1997; 'Slovenians Threaten General Strike in

'98', *St Petersburg Times*, 16 December 1997; 'World Bank Waters Down Russia's Private Pensions Plan', *St Petersburg Times*, 24 March 1998; Vadim Demchenko and Yulia Finogenova, 'Predvectniky Pensionnoy Reformy' ('Forthcoming Pension Reforms'), *Ekspert*, Moscow, no. 15, 20 April 1998; plus personal research in Slovakia, 1993–94, Bulgaria, 1996–97, Russia, 1998–99 and Albania, 1999.

12. 'Cultural' – over the much publicised disputes about the film and video industries in the GATT discussions; 'political' – over who has jurisdiction over broader European disputes such as the Balkan civil wars, as well as the 'enlargement' of the EU (non-American control) and NATO (American) into Central and Eastern Europe; this could lead to the development of competing security policies (see Nunn and Stulberg, 2000); 'economic' – concerning investment by US companies and pension funds in Europe, and the future role of the Euro single currency against the dollar. Martin Feldstein, former Reagan adviser, cited in the text for his arguments in favour of privatisation of pension arrangements, predicts increased conflict within Europe, and between Europe and the US, as a result of European Monetary Union. He suggests that this should lead to a realignment of US foreign policy now that there is no longer a 'common enemy'. The US can no longer 'count on' Europe, he concludes (Feldstein, 1997b).

13. Teresa Ghilarducci, 'The Many Faces of Union Pension Plans', ENRSP I, plus Ghilarducci, 1992, Barber and Ghilarducci, 1993. For Australia, Olsberg, 1994.

Bibliography

Achcar, Gilbert, 1998, 'The Strategic Triad: The United States, Russia and China', *New Left Review*, no. 228, March/April.

Advisory Council on Social Security, 1997, *Final Report of the 1994–1996 Advisory Council on Social Security*, vol. 1, *Findings and Recommendations*, Washington DC, Social Security Administration.

Altvater, Elmar, 1998, 'Theoretical Deliberations on Time and Space in Post-socialist Transformation', *Regional Studies*, vol. 32, no. 7.

AP Information Services, 1996, *Pension Funds and their Advisers*, London: AP Information Services.

Arrighi, Giovanni, 1994, *The Long Twentieth Century: Money, Power and the Origins of Our Times*, London: Verso.

Ascoli, Ugo, 1996, 'Retirement System Reform: Is Italy Moving Toward an Increasingly Minimal Welfare State?', ENRSP I.

Asher, Mukul, 1998, 'The Future of Retirement Protection in Southeast Asia', *International Social Security Review*, vol. 51, no. 1.

Bailey, Martin N., Diana Farrell and Susan Lund, 2000, 'The Color of Hot Money', *Foreign Affairs*, vol. 79, no. 2, March/April.

Banker, 1998, 'Behind the hedges', November, pp. 24–5.

Barber, Randy and Teresa Ghilarducci, 1993, 'Pension Funds, Long Term Investment and the Economic Future', in Gary Dimski, Gerald Epstein and Robert Pollin, eds, *Transforming the US*

Financial System: Equity and Efficiency for the 21st Century, New York: Armonk.

Beveridge, Sir William, 1966 reprint, *Social Insurance and Allied Services*, Cmd. 6404, London: HMSO.

Blackburn, Robin, 1999, 'The New Collectivism: Pension Reform, Grey Capitalism and Complex Socialism', *New Left Review*, no. 233, January/February.

——, 2000, 'How to Bring Back Collectivism', *New Statesman*, 17 January.

Bonoli, Giuloni, 1997, 'Classifying Welfare States: A Two-Dimensional Approach', *Journal of Social Policy*, vol. 20, no. 3, July.

Butler, E., M. Asher and K. Borden, 1995, *Singapore versus Chile: Competing Models for Welfare Reform*, London: Adam Smith Institute.

Butler, Rick, 1998, 'The Price of Pension Reform', *Institutional Investor*, April.

Campbell, Mary, 1998, 'Pensions; Redressing the Balance', *The Political Quarterly*, vol. 69, no. 1, January–March.

Caufield, Catherine, 1997, *Masters of Illusion: The World Bank and the Poverty of Nations*, London: Macmillan.

CEC (Commission of the European Communities), 1997, *Modernising and Improving Social Protection in the EU*, COM(97)102, Brussels: CEC.

Chapman, Stanley, 1984, *The Rise of Merchant Banking*, London: Allen and Unwin.

Commission on Social Justice, 1994 (the Borrie report), *Social Justice: Strategies for National Renewal*, London: Vintage.

Commission on Wealth Creation and Social Cohesion in a Free Society, 1995, *Report*, London: Commission on Wealth Creation.

Committee of Public Accounts, 1997, *The Elderly: Information Requirements for Supporting the Elderly and the Implications of Personal Pensions for the National Insurance Fund*, Eighth Report, London: HMSO.

Conrad, Christoph, 1994, *Vom Greis zum Rentner: Der Strukturwandel des*

Alters in Deutschland zwischen 1880 und 1930, Kritische Studien zur Geschichtswissenschaft, no. 104, Gottingen: Vandenhoek und Ruprecht.

Corbridge, Stuart, Ron Martin and Nigel Thrift, eds, 1994, *Money, Power and Space*, Oxford, UK, and Cambridge, USA: Blackwell.

Cordery, Adam, 1994, 'Foreign Capital Flows and Latin America: A Perspective on Recent Trends', *Business Economist*, vol. 25, no. 2, spring.

Council for Social Welfare, 1997, *Planning Pensions for All: A Response to the National Pensions Policy Initiative*, Dublin: Council for Social Welfare.

Crawford, Malcolm, 1997, 'The Big Pensions Lie', *New Economy*, vol. 4, issue 1, spring.

CSO (Central Statistical Office), 1993, 'Insurance Companies and Pension Fund Investment', *Business Monitor MQ5*, London: HMSO, January.

——, 1995, *Share Ownership: A Report on the Ownership of Shares at 31 December 1994*, London: HMSO.

Davies, Bryn, 2000, 'Equity Within and Between Generations', ENRSP II. [The article for which reference is made for the year 2000 was originally produced in 1996 (hence ENRSP II), but published in book form later. There is a further version of the Davies article in ENRSP V.]

Davis, E. P., 1993, 'The UK Fund Management Industry', *Business Economist*, 24(2).

——, 1995, *Pension Funds: Retirement-Income, Security, and Capital Markets: An International Perspective*, Oxford: Clarendon.

——, 1997, *Can Pension Systems Cope? Population Ageing, and Retirement Income Provision in the European Union*, London: Royal Institute of International Affairs.

Deacon, Bob, with Michelle Huber and Paul Stubbs, 1997, *Global Social Policy: International Organisations and the Future of Welfare*, London: Sage.

Dolowitz, David and David Marsh, 1996, 'Who Learns What from

Whom: A Review of the Policy Transfer Literature', *Political Studies*, vol. XLIV.

Dore, Ronald, William Lazonick and Mary O'Sullivan, 1999, 'Varieties of Capitalism in the Twentieth Century', *Oxford Review of Economic Policy*, vol. 15, no. 4, winter.

Drucker, Peter, 1976, *The Unseen Revolution: How Pension Fund Socialism Came to America*, Oxford: Oxford University Press.

——, 1997, 'The Global Economy and the Nation State', *Foreign Affairs*, vol. 76, no. 5, September/October.

Eberstadt, Nicholas, 1997, 'Too Few People?', *Prospect*, December.

Economist, 1998, 'Credit derivatives', 5 December.

——, 1999, 'The non-governmental order', 11 December.

EFRP (European Federation for Retirement Provision), 1996, *European Pension Funds; Their Impact on European Capital Markets and Competitiveness*, EC Green Paper, Brussels.

Esping-Andersen, Gøsta, 1990, *The Three Worlds of Welfare Capitalism*, New York: Polity Press.

——, 1994, 'Welfare States and the Economy', in N. J. Smelser and R. Swedburg, eds, *The Handbook of Economic Sociology*, Princeton: Princeton University Press.

——, ed., 1996, *Welfare States in Transition: National Adaptations in Global Economies*, London: Sage.

Fairmount, Frederic E., 1996, *The Rise and Fall of Economic Liberalism; The Making of the Economic Gulag*, Penang: Southbound and Third World Network.

Falkingham, Jane and Paul Johnson, 1996, 'Public Pensions and the Private Sector: a new way forward', *Soundings*, issue 4, autumn.

Feldstein, Martin, 1974, 'Social Security, Induced Retirement, and Aggregate Capital Formation', *Journal of Political Economy*, vol. 82, no. 5, September/October.

——, 1997a, 'The Case for Privatisation', *Foreign Affairs*, vol., 76, no. 4, July/August.

——, 1997b, 'EMU and International Conflict', *Foreign Affairs*, vol. 76, no. 6, November/December.

Field, Frank, 1996, *How to Pay for the Future*, London: Institute of Community Studies.

Financial Times, 1996a, Supplement: Pension Fund Investment, 2 May.

——, 1996b, 'A Boost for Capital Markets', 4 April.

——, 1998a, 'Hedge Fund Built Up Exposure to Market of $200 bn', 26 September, plus 'Banks Hit Again by Shock Waves from LTCM', 2 October.

——, 1998b, 'Lessons of the Asia Crisis', 12 December.

——, 1998c, 'Frail Orthodoxy', 21 October.

——, 1998d, 'World-wide Jitters Spur Stampede to Super-safe Havens', 6 October.

——, 1998e, ' Mother of Reinvention', 2 June.

——, 1998f, 'Pension Failures Add to the Japanese Sense of Economic Malaise', 17 June.

——, 1999a, 12 April.

——, 1999b, Survey of 'German Banking and Finance', 25 October.

——, 1999c, 'Greenspan Sees Little Gain from Social Security Plan', 4 March.

——, 2000a, 'Triumph for Vodafone as Mannesmann Gives In', 4 February, and 'Whirlwinds of Change', in 'Comment and Analysis' by John Plender, same date.

——, 2000b, 'Central Banks Warn of Global Hard Landing', 6 June.

——, 2000c, 'London Pressed to Hold Top Spot as Equity Centre', 13 June.

——, 2000d, 'Pension Payouts "Depend on Pot Luck"', Money Supplement, 16 June.

——, 2000e, 'Pension Moves May Boost Equity Flows', 30 June.

Fischer, Bernard, 1997, 'The Role of Contractual Savings Institutions in Emerging Markets', in *Institutional Investors in the New Financial Landscape*, Paris: OECD Proceedings.

Friot, Bernard, 1997, 'Social Contributions, Earmarked Taxes and Wage Earner Savings in the Financing of Social Protection; A Comparison between the British and French Systems', ENRSP III.

——, 1998a, 'Not-for-Profit Retirement: The Politics of Socialised Wages', ENRSP IV.

——, 1998b, *Puissances du salariat: emploi et protection sociale à la française*, Paris: La Dispute.

Ghilarducci, Teresa, 1992, *Labor's Capital: The Economics and Politics of Private Pensions*, Cambridge, Mass.: MIT Press.

——, 1996, 'The Many Faces of Union Pension Plans', ENRSP I.

Gillion, Colin, John Turner, Clive Bailey and Denis Latulippe, 2000, *Social Security Pensions; Development and Reform*, Geneva: International Labour Office, p. 320 (contribution by Bryn Davies).

Goddard, J. B., 1992, 'Structural Economic Change and the Regions', paper presented at the annual conference of the Regional Studies Association, London.

Goodin, Robert E., Bruce Heady, Ruud Muffels and Henk-Jan Dirven, 1999, *The Real Worlds of Welfare Capitalism*, Cambridge: Cambridge University Press.

Gordon, Margaret, 1988, *Social Security Policies in Industrial Countries: A Comparative Perspective*, Cambridge: Cambridge University Press.

Gough, Ian, 1996, 'Social Policy and Competitiveness', *New Political Economy*, vol. 1, no. 2.

Government Actuary, 1991, *Occupational Pension Schemes*, London: HMSO.

Grabel, Ilene, 1997, 'Savings, Investment and Functional Efficiency', in R. Pollin, ed., *The Macroeconomics of Saving, Finance and Investment*, Ann Arbor: University of Michigan Press.

Grahl, John and Paul Teague, 1997, 'Is the European Social Model Fragmenting?', *New Political Economy*, vol. 2, no. 3.

Guardian, 1998, 'A Tale of Two Catastrophes', 7 November.

Harmes, Adam, 1998, 'Institutional Investors and the Reproduction of NeoLiberalism', *Review of International Political Economy*, vol. 5, no. 1, spring.

Henwood, Doug, 1998, *Wall Street: How it Works and for Whom*, London: Verso.

HMSO, 1997, *Family Resources Survey, 1995–6*, London: HMSO.

Holzmann, Robert, 1997a, 'Starting Over in Pensions: The Challenges Facing Central and Eastern Europe', *Journal of Public Policy*, vol. 17, no. 3.

——, 1997b, 'Pension Reform, Financial Market Development and Economic Growth: Preliminary Evidence from Chile', *IMF Working Paper*, WP/96/94.

Huber, Evelyne, 1996, 'Options for Social Policy in Latin America: Neoliberal versus Social Democratic Models', in Esping-Andersen, 1996.

Hughes, Gerard, 2000, 'Pension Financing, the Substitution Effect and National Savings', ENRSP II.

IFC (International Finance Corporation – World Bank), 1996, *Emerging Stock Markets Fact Book*, Washington IFC.

——, 1998, *Emerging Stock Markets Fact Book*, Washington: IFC

IMF (International Monetary Fund), 1997, *International Capital Markets: Developments, Prospects and Key Policy Issues*, Washington, November.

——, 1998, *Hedge Funds and Financial Market Dynamics*, Occasional Paper 166, Washington, May.

Incomes Data Services, 1993, *Pensions Service Bulletin*, 7 November.

Institutional Investor, 1997, 'Worldly-wise asset allocation', January.

——, 1998, 'America's largest overseas investors', July.

International Herald Tribune, 2000, 'Wage Pact in Germany Sets Tone for National Deal', 29 March.

InterSec Research Corporation, 1994, *Global Briefing Service*, Greenwich, USA.

Jacot, Henri, 2000, 'An Unsuspected Collectivism', *New Left Review*, no. 1 (new series), January/February.

James, Estelle, 1996, 'Providing Better Protection and Promoting Growth; A Defence of Averting the Old Age Crisis', *International Social Security Review*, vol. 49, no. 3.

Johnson, Paul, 1994, *The Pensions Dilemma*, London: Commission for Social Justice, Institute for Public Policy Research (IPPR).

Judt, Tony, 1997, 'The Social Question Redivivus', *Foreign Affairs*, vol. 76, no. 5, September/October.

Kapstein, Ethan B., 1998, 'Reviving the State' (review of World Bank Development Report, 1997), *World Policy Journal*, vol. XV, no. 1, spring.

Kindleberger, Charles, P., 1996 edition, *Manias, Panics and Crashes: A History of Financial Crises*, New York: Wiley.

Leimer, Dean R. and Selig Lesnoy, 1982, 'Social Security and Private Saving: New Time Series Evidence', *Journal of Political Economy*, vol. 90, no. 3, June.

Leone, Richard, 1997, 'Stick with Public Pensions', *Foreign Affairs*, vol. 76, no. 4, July/August.

Lesnoy, Selig D. and Dean R. Leimer, 1987, 'Social Security and Private Saving; Theory and Historical Evidence', in Charles W. Meyer, ed., *Social Security; A Critique of Radical Reform Proposals*, Lexington, Massachusetts: Lexington Books.

Leyshon, Andrew, 1994, 'Under Pressure: Finance, Geo-economic Competition and the Rise and Fall of Japan's Postwar Growth Economy', in Corbridge et al., 1994.

Lips, Carrie, 1999, 'State and Local Government Retirement Programs: Lessons in Alternatives to Social Security', *Social Security Privatisation*, CATO Institute, SSP no. 16, 17 March.

Littlewood, Michael, 1998, *How to Create a Competitive Market in Pensions: The International Lessons*, London: IEA Health and Welfare Unit, Choice in Welfare no. 45.

Mackenzie, G. A., Philip Gerson and Alfredo Cuevas, 1997, *Pension Regimes and Saving*, IMF Occasional Paper 153, Washington, August.

Martin, Ron, 1994, 'Stateless Monies, Global Financial Integration and National Economic Autonomy: The End of Geography?' in Corbridge et al., 1994.

Martin, Ron and Richard Minns, 1995, 'Undermining the Financial Basis of Regions: The Structure and Implications of the UK Pension Fund System', *Regional Studies*, vol. 29, no. 2.

Mayer, Colin, 1988, 'New Issues in Corporate Finance', *European Economic Review*, no. 32.

Minns, Richard, 1980, *Pension Funds and British Capitalism, the Ownership and Control of Shareholdings*, London: Heinemann.

——, 1996a, 'The Social Ownership of Capital', *New Left Review*, no. 219, September/October.

——, 1996b, 'The Political Economy of Pensions', *New Political Economy*, vol. 1, no. 3.

——, 1997, 'Pulp Fiction: Pensioning Off the State', *Policy Paper*, no. 2, Political Economy Research Centre, University of Sheffield.

Minns, Richard and Ron Martin, 1994, 'Les Fonds de Pension en Royaume-Uni: Centralisation et Contrôle', *Revue d'IRES*, 15.

Minns, Richard and John Tomaney, 1995, 'Regional Government and Local Economic Development: The Realities of Economic Power in the UK', *Regional Studies*, vol. 29, no. 2.

Minsky, H. P., 1989, 'Financial Crises and the Evolution of Capitalism; the Crash of '87 – What Does it Mean?' in M. Gottdiener and N. Komminos (eds), *Capitalist Development and Crisis Theory: Accumulation, Regulation and Spatial Restructuring*, New York: St Martin's Press.

Mitchell, Olivia S., Robert J. Myers and Howard Young, 1999, eds, *Prospects for Social Security Reform*, Pension Research Council, Wharton School of the University of Pennsylvania, Philadelphia: University of Pennsylvania Press.

Moody, Kim, 1997, 'Towards an International-Social Movement Unionism', *New Left Review*, no. 225, September/October.

Morgenson, Gretchen, 1999, 'Stocks and Social Security: Private Investors Do Better', *International Herald Tribune*, 25 January, p. 12.

Morris, Charles, 1999, *Money, Greed and Risk: Why Financial Crises and Crashes Happen*, Chichester: John Wiley & Sons.

Morris-Suzuki, Tessa, 2000, 'For and Against NGOs', *New Left Review*, no. 2 (new series), March/April.

Myles, John, 1996, 'When Markets Fail: Social Welfare in Canada and the United States', in Esping-Andersen, 1996.

Myles, John and Paul Pierson, 1998, 'The Comparative Political Economy of Pension Reform', paper presented at workshop on

'The New Politics of the Welfare State', Cambridge, Mass., October.

New Statesman, 1996, 'Interview with Peter Davis, Chief Executive of the Pru', 25 October.

Nunn, Sam and Adam N. Stulberg, 2000, 'The Many Faces of Modern Russia', *Foreign Affairs*, vol. 79, no. 2, March/April.

Observer, 1999, 'Forget Thatcher. Who'll Be the Biggest Privatiser of Them All?', 7 March.

OECD (Organisation for Economic Co-operation and Development), 1997, *Financial Market Trends*, no. 68, Paris: OECD.

——, 1998a, *Maintaining Prosperity in an Ageing Society*, Paris: OECD.

——, 1998b, 'International Financial Market Implications of Ageing Populations', *Financial Market Trends*, no. 71, Paris: OECD.

——, 1998c, 'Ageing Induced Capital Flows to Emerging Markets do not Solve the Basic Pension Problem in the OECD Area', *Financial Market Trends*, no. 70, Paris: OECD.

Office of National Statistics, 1997, *Financial Statistics*, February, London: HMSO.

Oling, Christina, 2000, 'The Effects of a Fully Funded Pension System on Individual Savings Behaviour', ENRSP II.

Olsberg, Diana, 1994, 'Australia's Retirement Income Revolution: A New Model for Retirement Savings and Investment Politics', *Economic and Industrial Democracy*, vol. 15.

——, 1995, 'Australia's Retirement Income Revolution: A Finnish System Down-Under', *Scandinavian Journal of Social Welfare*, vol. 4.

Orszag, Peter R. and Joseph E. Stiglitz, 1999, 'Rethinking Pension Reform: Ten Myths about Social Security Systems', Paper presented to the conference on 'New Ideas about Social Security', World Bank, Washington DC, 14–15 September.

Peterson, Peter G., 1999, 'Gray Dawn: The Global Aging Crisis', *Foreign Affairs*, vol. 78, no. 1, January/February.

Pfefferman, G., 1988, *Private Business in Developing Countries*, IFC Discussion Paper, no. 1, Washington DC: World Bank.

Pollin, Robert, ed., 1997, *The Macroeconomics of Saving, Finance and Investment*, Ann Arbor: University of Michigan Press.

Porter, Michael and Mark Kramer, 1999, 'Philanthropy's New Agenda: Creating Value', *Harvard Business Review*, November/December.

Reynaud, Emmanuel, 1994, *Les Retraites en France; le rôle des régimes complémentaires*, Paris: La Documentation Française.

Rybczynski, T., 1988, 'Financial Systems and Industrial Restructuring', *Nat West Bank Quarterly Review*, November.

Siaroff, A., 1994, 'Work, Women and Gender Equality: A New Typology,' in David Sainsbury, ed., *Gendering Welfare States*, London: Sage.

Singh, Ajit, 1995, *Corporate Financial Patterns in Industrialising Economies: A Comparative International Study*, Technical Paper for the IFC, Washington DC: World Bank.

——, 1996, 'Pension Reform, the Stock Market, Capital Formation and Economic Growth: A Critical Commentary on the World Bank's Proposals', *International Social Security Review*, vol. 49, no. 3.

Singh, Ajit and Bruce A. Weisse, 1998, 'Emerging Stock Markets, Portfolio Capital Flows and Long-term Economic Growth: Micro- and Macroeconomic Perspectives', *World Development*, vol. 26, no. 4, April.

Sklair, Leslie, 1997, 'Social Movements for Globalisation; the Transnational Capitalist Class in Action', *Review of International Political Economy*, vol. 4, no. 3, autumn.

Steinmeyer, Heinz-Dietrich, 1999, 'Tax Treatment of Supplementary Pensions in Germany', ENRSP V.

Sunstein, Cass R. 1997, *Free Markets AND Social Justice*, Oxford: Oxford University Press.

Thrift, Nigel, Andrew Leyshon and Peter Daniels, 1987, '"Sexy Greedy": The New International Financial System, the City of London and the South East of England', Working Paper on Producer Services no. 8, Universities of Bristol and Liverpool.

Titmuss, Richard, 1973, *The Gift Relationship: From Human Blood to Social Policy*, London: Penguin.

——, 1974, *Social Policy*, London: Allen and Unwin.

——, 1976, *The Commitment to Welfare*, London: Allen and Unwin.

Treisman, Daniel, 1996, 'The Politics of Intergovernmental Transfers in Post-Soviet Russia', *British Journal of Political Science*, vol. 26.

UNCTAD (United Nations Conference on Trade and Development), 1999, *World Investment Report 1999; Foreign Direct Investment and the Challenge of Development*, New York and Geneva: United Nations.

UNDP (United Nations Development Project), 1999a, *Human Development Report 1999*, New York: UNDP.

——, 1999b, 'Message from the Administrator', *Cooperation South*, no. 1, June, New York: UNDP Special Unit for Technical Cooperation Among Developing Countries.

UPS (Union Pension Services), 1993, 1996, 2000, *Pension Scheme Profiles*, London: Union Pension Services.

van Reisen, Mirjam, 1999, 'EU "Global Player", The North South Policy of the European Union', paper presented to conference on 'International NGOs, Consulting Companies and Global Social Policy; Subcontracting Governance?', Helsinki, December 1999, organised by GASSP (Globalisation and Social Policy Programme, Helsinki National Research and Development Centre for Welfare and Health, Finland, and Sheffield University Department of Sociological Studies, UK).

Vittas, Dimitri and Augusto Iglesias, 1992, 'The Rationale and Performance of Personal Pension Plans in Chile', *Policy Research Working Papers*, WPS 867, Washington DC: World Bank.

Wade, Robert and Frank Veneroso, 1998, 'The Asian Crisis: The High Debt Model versus the Wall Street-Treasury-IMF Complex', *New Left Review*, no. 228, March/April.

Wall Street Journal Europe, 1999, 1 September.

Weiss, Linda, 1997, 'Globalisation and the Myth of the Powerless State', *New Left Review*, no. 225, September/October.

Whiteford, Peter and Stephen Kennedy, 1995, *Income and Living Standards of Older People*, UK Department of Social Security, Research Report no. 34, London: HMSO.

Williamson, John B. and Fred C. Pampel, 1993, *Old-Age Security in Comparative Perspective*, New York: Oxford University Press.

Willmore, Larry, 1998, 'Social Security and the Provision of Retirement Income', Mimeograph, New York: United Nations.

World Bank, 1994, *Averting the Old Age Crisis: Policies to Protect the Old and Promote Growth*, New York: Oxford University Press.

——, 1995, *Annual Report*, Washington DC: International Bank for Reconstruction and Development/World Bank.

——, 1997a, *Private Capital Flows to Developing Countries: The Road to Financial Integration*, New York: Oxford University Press.

——, 1997b, *Old Age Security; Pension Reform in China*, Washington DC: World Bank.

——, 1998, *Global Development Finance*, Washington DC: International Bank for Reconstruction and Development/World Bank.

Zysman, J., 1993, *Governments, Markets and Growth; Financial Systems and the Politics of Change*, Ithaca: Cornell University Press.

Index